INTO KOKERBOOM COUNTRY

Kokerbome or Quiver trees

Tree-like aloes (botanical name dichotoma) which grow on the hot northern slopes of the hills around Springbok, south to Garies and north into Namibia.

LOUIS VAN HEERDE COLLECTION

Springtime in Namaqualand

Picnics were a way of life brought to Namaqualand by the Cornish miners in the mid-1850s. This photo, taken around 1930, epitomises the happy atmosphere of picnics in the veld and the 'pursuit of happiness' that Abe Schapera, one-time resident and chronicler of Jewish life in Namaqualand, writes about. Amongst them, (top) Milly Gelb, Harold Gelb, Jack Sovinsky, Sybil Sovinsky, Bessie Jowell (bottom) Florrie Caplan, Caple Caplan, Milly Saharin, Lynton Rabie, Max Shapiro.

LULU RABIE COLLECTION

▶ Pioneers

Esther de Pass, the first Jewess; Rebecca (Bessie) Jowell, the last Jewess; and Paul Kahn, an early entrepreneur.

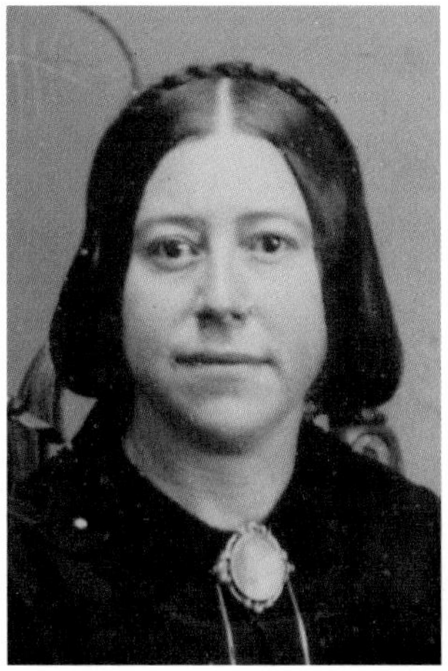

INTO KOKERBOOM COUNTRY

NAMAQUALAND'S JEWISH PIONEERS

PHYLLIS JOWELL AND ADRIENNE FOLB

FERNWOOD
PRESS

Traditional matjieshuis

A typical *matjieshuis* or reed mat house unique to Namaqualand. *LOUIS VAN HEERDE COLLECTION*

TO CECIL JOWELL

unstinting supporter of this project and most valued contributor:
our heartfelt thanks for your encouragement, insights and
willingness to read through countless manuscripts.
Without your input this book would never have reached fruition.

CONTENTS

Namaqualand
SOUTH AFRICA
NAMIBIA
Atlantic Ocean
NORTHERN CAPE
RICHTERSVELD
BUSHMANLAND
KNERSVLAKTE
Orange River
To Upington
Oranjemund
Alexander Bay
Vioolsdrift
Pella
Pofadder
Aggeneys
Anenous Pass
Steinkopf
Port Nolloth
Specktakel
Buffels River
Okiep
Concordia
Nababeep
Carolusberg
Springbok
Grootmis
Kleinsee
Komaggas
Lewerberg
Messelpad Pass
Bowesdorp
Soebatsfontein
Kamiesberg Pass
Gamoep
Kamieskroon
Kamiesberge
Hondeklipbaai
Wallekraal
Leliefontein
Garies
Bitterfontein
Nuwerus
Loeriesfontein
Nieuwoudtville
100 Kilometres
50 Miles
29
30
31
32
16
17
18
19

A COINCIDENCE

This book arose out of some of the interesting material that was accumulated during the course of our research for background information for the publication *Joe Jowell of Namaqualand* (published in 1994). It struck us vividly that a number of immigrant pioneering Jews had made their way to this remote and arid place at the turn of the twentieth century and carved out lives for themselves there.

With a determination to succeed, they established themselves in businesses, trades and professions and contributed to the welfare of the place. They married and raised their families and, importantly, maintained a commitment to their Jewish traditions, far from their roots. Their story is remarkable and inspiring and, in many respects, reflects Jewish country life in much of South Africa and perhaps also, immigrant groups generally.

Everyone involved in this project – ourselves, our professional assistants, the people we interviewed – has been fascinated by the emerging story of the Jews of Namaqualand.

The description of a visit to a Jewish resident in Port Nolloth in the 1850s which appears in *John Blades Currey, 1850 to 1900,*[1] has intrigued us for some time:

The Port Nolloth house

The Port Nolloth house built by Aaron de Pass in the early 1850s. Photograph taken 1996.

> It was dark when I reached Port Nolloth next evening and I was about dead-beat with weariness, hunger and thirst, but I had an old friend living there whose knowledge and appreciation of the pleasures of the table were famous and for some hours I had been gloating in imagination over a preliminary brandy and soda, a warm bath, a good dinner and a soft bed; so my surprise may be imagined when I was not even admitted into his house. But presently he came out and explained that I had most unfortunately arrived just as the Great White Fast commenced, the observance of which by people of the Jewish faith is obligatory and that, moreover, his wife who was strict in such matters was with him and that in short he could not receive me.

John Blades Currey was manager of the Namaqua Copper Mining Company at that time (September 1856) and had been in Hondeklip Bay on his 'usual monthly business'. Called urgently to Port Nolloth to examine the wreck of a vessel belonging to the company, he had spent all day riding there. Instead of the comforts he had hoped for, he had to sleep in an outside room and wait until the next evening when, after his friend had sighted the first star which heralded the end of the fast, he was enthusiastically invited in for a hot meal of turkey.

Over the years, we have tried to trace the man to whom John Blades Currey was referring. We knew that there were only two or three houses in Port Nolloth at that time. We also knew from the diaries of one Aaron de Pass, an English Jew, that he had travelled extensively in Namaqualand with his wife during that decade and had business interests there. It was our first intimation of a Jew in the region. It was only some eight years into our research that the mystery was solved. Arlene Fanaroff, researching this story for us, went to the Deeds Office in Cape Town and returned with a copy of the official government record of the owners of Erf No. 93 in Port Nolloth. The record shows that on 20 July 1855, this erf was granted to Aaron de Pass. In the isolated, coastal village of Port Nolloth, far from the nearest Jewish community, this Jewish couple, Aaron and Esther de Pass, were observing the enduring tradition of *Yom Kippur*.

There have been only three owners of that property: the first, Aaron de Pass, the first Jew in Namaqualand; the second, the Cape Copper Company Limited and the third, Joseph Jowell who together with his wife were the last Jews to be buried in Namaqualand.

Call it coincidence. Call it fate. Or call it vibrant testimony of a long and meaningful association that Namaqualand's Jews have had with this unlikely homeland. The years between Aaron and Esther de Pass and Joseph and Rebecca Jowell represent a remarkable era and a story that must be told.

Phyllis Jowell
Adrienne Folb

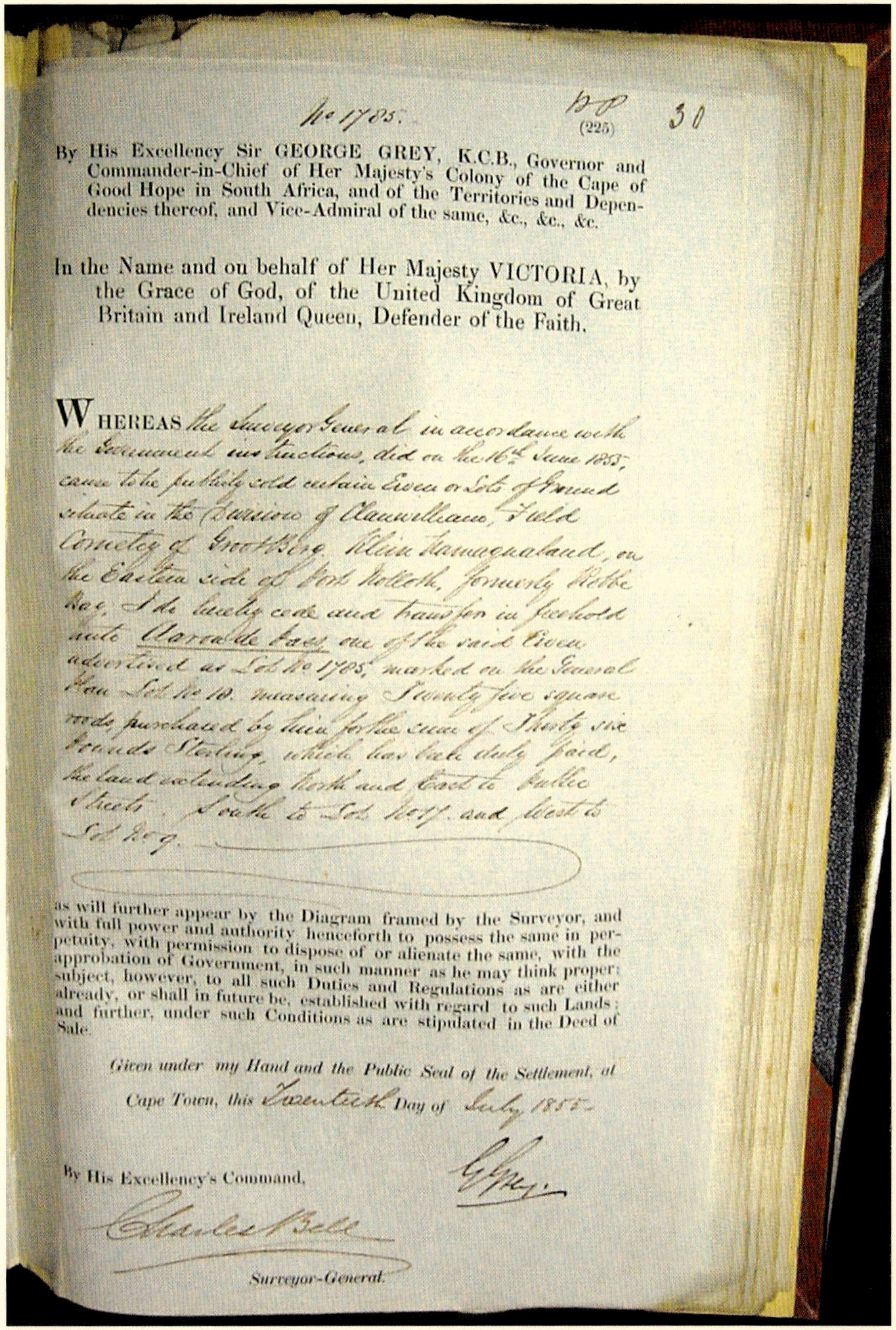

No 1785. DP (225) 30

By His Excellency Sir GEORGE GREY, K.C.B., Governor and Commander-in-Chief of Her Majesty's Colony of the Cape of Good Hope in South Africa, and of the Territories and Dependencies thereof, and Vice-Admiral of the same, &c., &c., &c.

In the Name and on behalf of Her Majesty VICTORIA, by the Grace of God, of the United Kingdom of Great Britain and Ireland Queen, Defender of the Faith.

WHEREAS the Surveyor General in accordance with the Government instructions, did on the 16th June 1855, cause to be publicly sold certain Erven or Lots of Ground situate in the Division of Clanwilliam, Field Cornetcy of Grootberg, Klein Namaqualand, on the Eastern side of Port Nolloth, formerly Robbe Bay, I do hereby cede and transfer in freehold unto Aaron de Pass one of the said Erven advertised as Lot No 1785, marked on the General Plan Lot No 10. measuring Twenty five square roods purchased by him for the sum of Thirty six Pounds Sterling, which has been duly paid, the land extending North and East to Public Streets. South to Lot No 7. and West to Lot No 9.

as will further appear by the Diagram framed by the Surveyor, and with full power and authority henceforth to possess the same in perpetuity, with permission to dispose of or alienate the same, with the approbation of Government, in such manner as he may think proper: subject, however, to all such Duties and Regulations as are either already, or shall in future be, established with regard to such Lands; and further, under such Conditions as are stipulated in the Deed of Sale.

Given under my Hand and the Public Seal of the Settlement, at Cape Town, this Twentieth *Day of* July 1855.

G Grey

By His Excellency's Command,

Charles Bell

Surveyor-General.

Deed of Sale

Deed of Sale of the Port Nolloth house owned originally by Aaron and Esther de Pass and finally by Joseph and Rebecca Jowell. Currently it remains the holiday home of the Jowell family.

1 THE PIONEERS ARRIVE

The presence of Jewish pioneers in Namaqualand spans more than a hundred years, with the first Jew, Aaron de Pass, arriving in 1851 and the last Jew, Rebecca Jowell, being buried there in 1987. The Jewish population peaked during the 1930s with approximately 200 people carving out a life and making a mark in this remote and arid region of South Africa. There were few families who stayed for more than two generations – many stayed for only one, moving to the cities in order to further their prospects. Despite their small numbers, their influence on the cultural, community and economic history of the area is significant, and, according to Theunis Uys, a native Namaqualander, an integral part of Namaqualand history.[1]

The Namaqualand Jews came from towns in England, Wales and Germany and the *shtetlekh* (villages) of Eastern Europe. After 1881 the main wave of Jewish immigration was primarily from the Pale of Settlement, which comprised parts of Russian Poland, Lithuania and south and southwest Russia. The Jews who left Eastern Europe at that time were fleeing impossible tyrannical economic conditions and persecutions or *pogroms* which followed the assassination of Tsar Alexander II in 1881. In addition there was the discriminatory practice of military conscription for Jewish boys. At the age of twelve all Jewish boys were conscripted for a period of 25 years; each Jewish community was given a quota and sometimes boys of eight or nine were kidnapped by professional 'snatchers' (*khapers* in Yiddish) to meet the quota. Once in the army they were beaten into submission and forced to convert to Russian Orthodoxy.[2] The discovery of gold on the Witwatersrand in 1886 was therefore a major draw-card for Jews looking for opportunities elsewhere. Historians record that at least 70 000 Jews are believed to have entered South Africa between 1881 and 1930 when the Quota Act restricting their entry was promulgated.[3]

On the whole, the pattern of immigration to Namaqualand followed the general pattern of the Jews who went to live in other *platteland* (rural) regions of South Africa. These new Jewish immigrants dispersed to hundreds of small towns and villages, wherever they could make a living, often following relatives or fellow countrymen who had come from the same villages as they had in the Old Country.

They came with very little in the way of money or possessions. They often started as *smouse*, (itinerant pedlars), working very hard to achieve their financial objectives. They brought out family members who assisted them in their endeavours – wives, brothers, brothers-in-law, cousins and nephews. The family was the core of their existence – their emotional, social, communal and economic support. They joined forces with other Jews in the area and established Jewish institutions, at first informally when their numbers were small, and then formally when their numbers had swelled. They were Zionists first and foremost and established Zionist Societies even before they established religious congregations. They cared for their own community as well as becoming involved in the welfare and activities of the community at large.[4]

The Jewish immigrants were people who looked for the gap. Where there was a need, they found their opportunities. In Lithuania they were involved in commercial activities such as shopkeeping, farming, hotel keeping, transportation and trading. In those regions

◀ **Smous with cart**

Jewish immigrants first appeared in Namaqualand in the late 1880s as *smouse* or itinerant pedlars to service the communities of farmers, miners, mission stations and villages. Smousing was a way of earning a living for many early immigrants, including Jews.
SA Friends of Beth Hatefutsoth

Smous in Upington

This photo, taken in Upington, portrays a fairly typical scene which would be played out when the *smous* (on the far right of this picture) arrived in the community with his wagon full of wares and locals gathered to shop.
South African Jewish Museum

where the local farmers raised sheep and cattle, and where there were leather-works in the town, the Jewish pedlars traded skins directly with the farmers. They also traded in furs and pastoral products. The *smous* in South Africa fulfilled a similar need, first as a supplier of the necessities, and sometimes the small luxuries, that isolated farming couples could not acquire by simply going down to the shops as was the case with their urban counterparts. Farming families, the *smous* soon found out, had problems in disposing of produce in small lots that did not warrant a trek to the nearest town, and also had a shortage of cash as a result. So the *smous* bartered his goods for farm produce. Many of them ended up starting small shops themselves. Similarly, Jewish hoteliers saw opportunities to provide hospitality to travellers and thus established country hotels. The Jewish immigrants were creative and hard working and had learned the quality of endurance through many centuries of persecution.

What attracted the Jews to Namaqualand were the opportunities offered by the development of copper mining in the 1850s and the lure of diamonds during the 1920s. The resulting increase in population created a corresponding increase in the demand for goods and services. Jewish immigrants recognized the economic potential of such activities and became the middlemen minority of the region – smousing, trading, shopkeeping and hotel keeping – rather than becoming involved in the mining itself.[5] Their activities were not so dissimilar from those in their erstwhile homeland. They did not come to get rich quickly, as did the speculators in the copper rush of the 1850s, but in order to make a

Levy's shop in Nababeep

Levy's store in Nababeep circa 1911. The owner of the store was Maurice Levy who opened a chain of five stores in the area at the end of the nineteenth century. On the right was the butchery and in the centre, the general dealer's store. The brick building on the left still stands today and is used as a mining museum.
David Levy collection

living. Theunis Uys, whose family had been in the area since the late 1800s, has given a detailed and appreciative description of the early Jewish settlers in his unpublished memoirs:

> *Saam met hierdie mense het ook die Jodemense na Namaqualand gekom. Maar hulle het nie gekom om te kom myn of om gou ryk te word, nee hulle het gekom om te bly, om te oorleef, want hulle was almal brandarm. Hulle het gekom om biesnies te doen, te koep en te verkoep (sic) en te maak 'n klein bietjie profyt!* [6]

Later Jews who came to the area were tailors, bookkeepers, jewellers, lawyers, mineral prospectors, farmers, engineers, pharmacists, doctors, dentists, garage owners and transport operators, who provided more professional services.[7] They became vital members of the Namaqualand communities and a key influence in the development of the region.

The story of the Jews of Namaqualand is remarkable, and worth telling, not only for its rich cultural history and moral substance, but also for the lasting impact that these people made, both on the local area and on South Africa as a whole. For this is not simply the story of one remote and arid place. The Namaqualand Jewish story is the South African Jewish story: its trials, triumphs, challenges and joys represent those of Jewish brethren throughout the country and is, indeed, the story of many immigrant populations throughout the world. It is a microcosm of how a minority group transformed its own economic situation and left '*diep spore*' (deep imprints) on a faraway land.[8]

Saam met hierdie ... : 'Together with these people (the speculators) came the Jewish people. But they did not come to mine or to get rich quickly, they came to stay, to survive, because they were dirt poor. They came to do a little business, to buy and sell and to make a small profit.'

Early map of South Africa

Early map of South Africa by Guy Tachard published in Paris in 1686. It was drawn by Hendrik Claudius, an apothecary and naturalist, who accompanied Simon van der Stel, Commander of the Cape under Dutch East India Company rule, on his historic expedition to Namaqualand in 1685.
Norwich Oscar, Kolbe Pam. Maps of Africa. Johannesburg, 1983

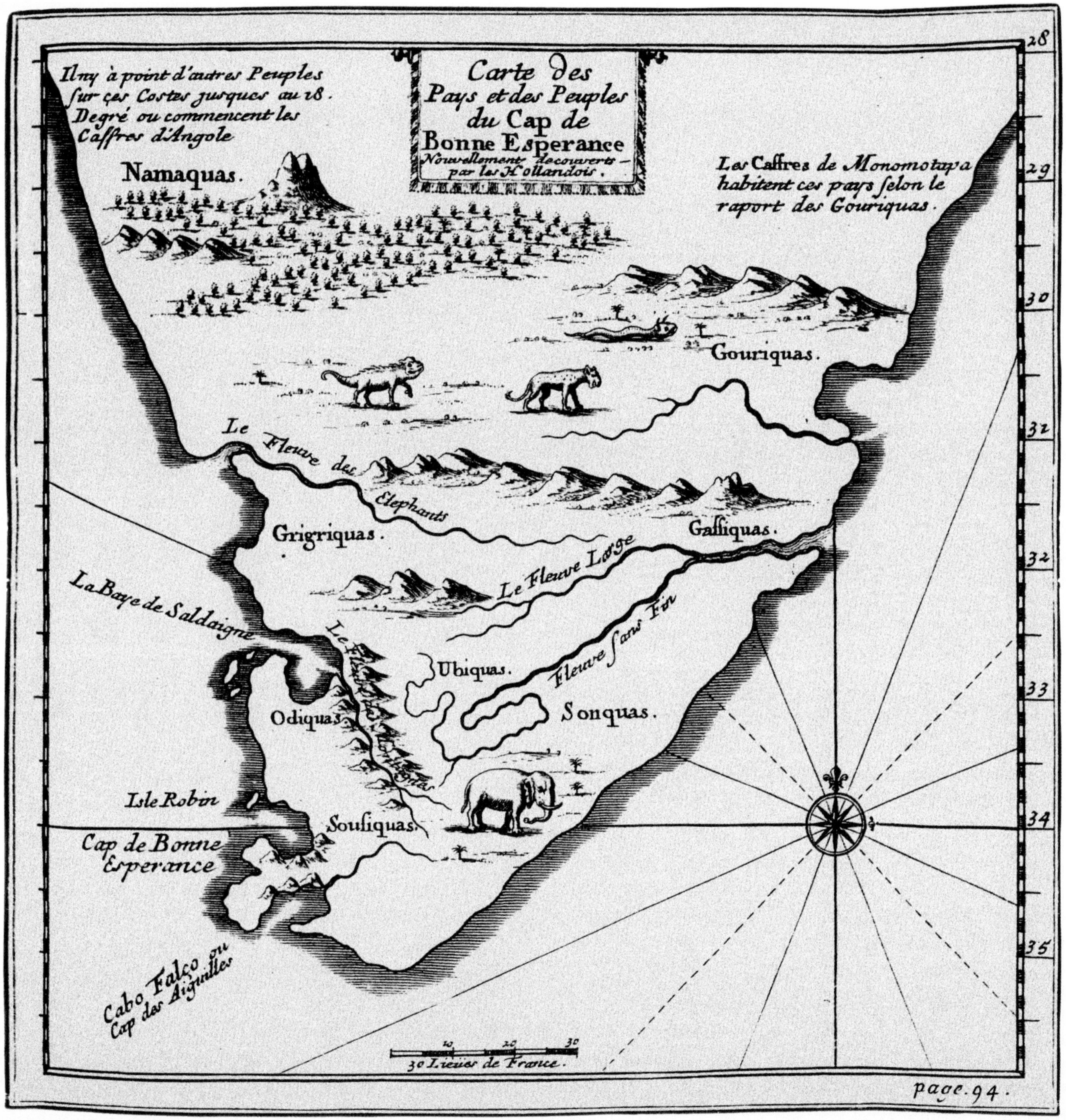

2 A TIMELESS LANDSCAPE

The Copper Mountain, 1685

Early sketch of the 'Copper Mountain' drawn in October 1685 by Hendrik Claudius during his expedition to Namaqualand. The indicators and letters on the sketch clearly show the mountains surrounding van der Stel's encampment, green with copper deposits.
Iziko Museums of Cape Town

Namaqualand is the semi-desert area situated in the north-western Cape often referred to as 'Little Namaqualand', in order to distinguish it from 'Great Namaqualand', formerly South West Africa, now Namibia. Hilly, sandy, waterless and mountainous, it has been described as an 'inhospitable area'. Its western boundary is the Atlantic Ocean; the northern boundary is the Orange River; the southern boundary has variously been defined as the Buffels River or a point 72 kilometres north of the Olifants River mouth; and on the east side, Bushmanland 'petering out somewhere near Upington'.[1]

Geologically, Namaqualand is considered one of the oldest parts of earth, with scientists dating some rocks on the banks of the Orange River as far back as two billion years. One billion years ago, Namaqualand was buried twenty kilometres below the earth's surface. Granites and gneisses, buried at depth, melted, mixed, crystallised, cooled and then thrust up over time, formed the distinctive features of Namaqualand – the coastal lowlands, the mountain belt through the Spectakel pass onwards to the Kamiesberg and the plateau of Bushmanland. Copper was formed then at the very deepest levels of the earth's crust at very high temperatures caused by the rise of molten magma from even greater depths. This copper is of a very high grade, although the tonnages are low, the metal being dispersed in hundreds of small bodies throughout what is known as the O'okiep copper district.[2] One such body, the Koperberg, drew the earliest European explorers into the mountainous interior of Namaqualand.

It was Simon van der Stel, Commander of the Cape under Dutch East India Company rule who, on orders from the Company to search for the mineral, set out on a five-month journey to 'the land of the Namaquas', and discovered copper in the 'Koperbergen' in 1685.[3] Shallow excavations at the site today tell the story of his discovery. Previous expeditions, not as well equipped as his, were unsuccessful because of the severe conditions encountered: 'a country … so parched with drought that it was impossible to proceed … impassable mountains …'. Van der Stel himself reported 'unbelievably high mountains'; rocky soil with 'much sand between them; high rocky mountains … kloofs with loose rocks …'.[4] He was pleased with the good grade copper ('lovely minerals') they dug out of the copper mountain but was unable to find a favourable route to transport it to the sea.

Local Khoi, richly adorned with copper jewellery

Local Khoi had been observed wearing copper jewellery by passing sailors on their way to the East as early as 1497. This Khoi family, particularly the woman (opposite), is depicted wearing numerous copper bracelets and chains. *Rijksmuseum collection, Amsterdam*

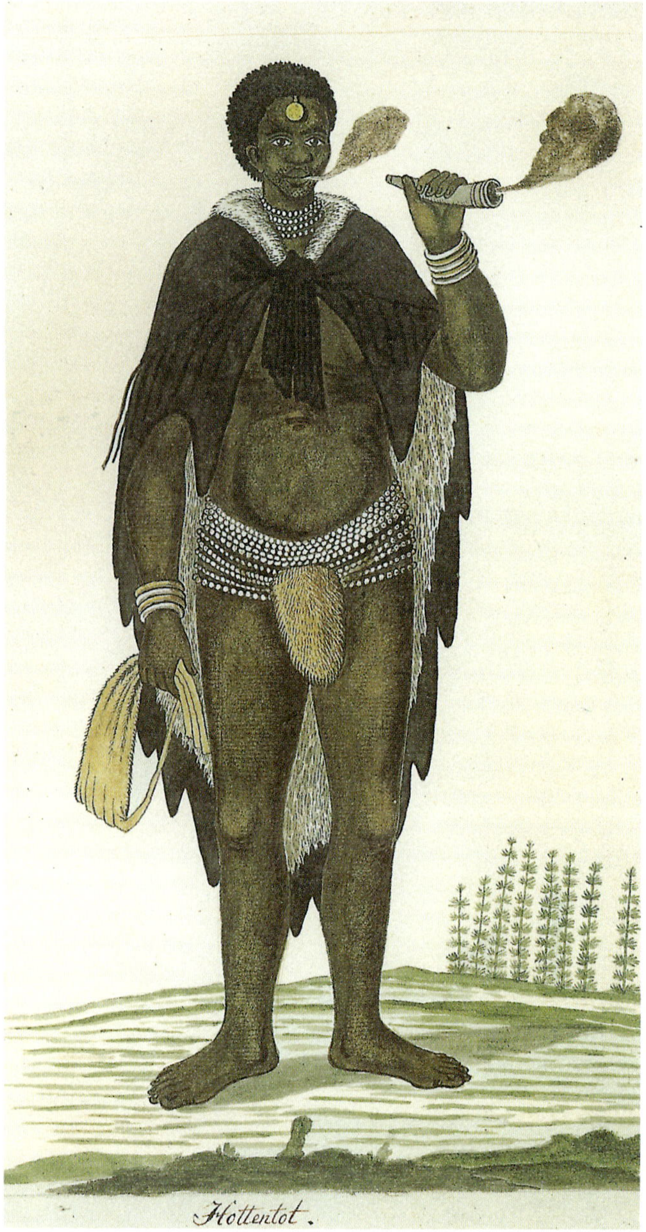

The terrain was either sandy or rocky; what little water there was, was brackish; the shore was rocky or there were sandbanks and the surf was very rough; the heat was terrible. In all, his assessment was that conditions were quite unsuitable for a viable exploration of the ore.[5] (Little did he know that below the sandy surface of the shoreline, richer than all the copper they had discovered, were fabulous quantities of diamonds!)[6] It would be nearly two hundred years before the copper was mined commercially.

Simon van der Stel may not have been successful in finding a way to exploit the copper resources of the area, but his expedition is considered important for pioneering contact between the new settlers and the indigenous people in the north-western part of the Cape. There he encountered the Hottentots or Khoi (whom he called 'Amaquas')[7] and their chiefs and traded brandy, tobacco and food for sheep, cattle and milk.

After Van der Stel, livestock traders, hunters, botanists and explorers journeyed to the territory in increasing numbers. Men such as William Paterson, the young Scottish botanist, visited the area from 1777 to 1779; Robert Jacob Gordon, Commander of the Dutch garrison at the Cape, in 1777 and 1779; François le Vaillant, ornithologist and naturalist in 1781; Sir John Barrow in 1798 and the Rev James Backhouse, the missionary, who visited Namaqualand in 1844; all recorded their travels in diaries and journals which added to the knowledge of the area, its geography and its peoples. Gordon, for instance, described the peoples he encountered, the Khoi and San, the Strandlopers; animals such as hippopotamuses, rhinoceroses, ostriches and giraffe; and plant life such as euphorbia and kokerbome.[8] Gordon ventured as far north as the Gariep River which he renamed the Orange River.[9]

The peoples encountered by these early travellers were ancient peoples, the first to inhabit South Africa. The San hunter-gatherers ('Bushmen') had come down from the north as early as the eighth century, followed by their kin, the Khoikhoi pastoralists.[10] At the Orange

River, the various Khoikhoi groups split up. The Namaquas, one branch, were drawn to the dry western part of Little Namaqualand which, with its nutritious succulent plants, was suitable for sheep farming (although they kept cattle and goats as well). They were also attracted by the cool climate, lovely spring water and melting snow-caps of the Kamiesberg. Like the San, who followed the huge herds of springbok as well as ostriches, giraffes and elephants, they made their way through the valleys and *kloofs* (ravines) of Namaqualand to the watering holes.

The Namaquas were first encountered by the Dutch colonists near the Fort of Good Hope in 1660, probably venturing there, according to Winifred Tucker 'to see what was going on and whom the strange people were who were willing to give such curious and delightful things in return for their superfluous cattle'. They were described as very tall people who wore 'all kinds of beads' and lived in mat houses; they kept goats and their household utensils were hollowed out tankards, calabashes and wooden vessels; they wore copper and iron chains and beads and prepared skins and hides; their weapons were assegais, bows and arrows. Later Simon van der Stel found them very friendly and extremely musical.[11]

By 1761 an expedition led by Hendrik Hop to the northern interior of the Colony found them in an impoverished condition, robbed by the San of the greater part of their cattle and subservient to the Dutch colonists. This process of decline had begun with the conflict of interests between the Namaquas, who were pastoralists, and the nomadic San. There were ongoing feuds especially in the area of the Orange River.[12] The relations between the Namaquas and the Cape Khoikhoi involved conflict as well, but the two groups also traded with one another and established important economic links,[13] trading in cattle, sheep and goats and, of cardinal importance to the Khoikhoi, iron and copper.[14]

But it was the advent of the Dutch *trekboers* (nomadic farmers) in the area that would herald the

Little Namaqualand, circa 1841

This watercolour by Charles Davidson Bell shows the *matjieshuis*, the traditional abode of indigenous people in the region. It was made from reeds woven into mats, thrown over a reed frame.
MuseumAfrika collection

demise of these ancient people. This new wave of settlers in the early 1700s were poor, nomadic men who had trekked north from the Cape to escape from the discipline of Dutch East India Company rule. They were a tenacious and independent breed of men searching for new grazing land and a better livelihood. There was a Company prohibition on trading in livestock with the Khoikhoi, but within half a century many of the free burgers had in fact become stock-farmers and had started moving away from the restrictive rule of the Cape. By the time Simon van der Stel arrived to take up his post as second Commander of the Cape Colony in 1679, the tendency to trek was well established. The system of grazing licenses, at first communal and then individual, developed into a system of loan farms and it was this system of land tenure which, more than any other factor, produced the trek farmer. Even the quitrent system introduced in 1732, which guaranteed the farmer occupation of land for at least 15 years after which, if the land reverted to the Company, the farmer would be paid the value of all fixed improvements, failed to discourage trekking. The enormous distances, lack of roads and a shortage of officials hampered control of these farmers by the authorities at the Cape.

As the *trekboers* fanned out ever deeper into the interior, they encountered the Khoikhoi and San. There was bound to be conflict over land because the concept of individual land ownership was unknown to the

Khoikhoi. For them, land belonged to the community. So the Khoikhoi and San fell back before the *trekboers*. In the end, writes Nigel Penn, the Khoikhoi were defeated and the San virtually exterminated. Captured children were reared as servants. Some Namaquas elected to stay alongside the new white intruders who settled in the area on their large and widely scattered farms, far away from the amenities at the Cape. Miscegenation took place and the children of these relationships, sometimes marriages, were termed 'Basters'. The children were virtually all assimilated into the Khoikhoi society. [15]

The *trekboers* lived simple lives. On their grazing land their homes were huts with mud walls and reed roofs. Sometimes they merely lived under their wagons with a canvas awning alongside the wagon. Khoisan servants tended the flocks and herds, so the men were free to go hunting, an occupation that provided them with ivory and skins for barter on rare visits to town. Wives and servants tended small gardens that produced vegetables just sufficient for the needs of the household. Once a year the farmer and his family would make the journey to the Cape to trade, sell animals, have children baptised and stock up on essentials such as lead, gunpowder, coffee, tea and sugar.[16]

By about 1750 the first farms had been leased in the Kamiesberge with Leliefontein and Groenrivier the favoured areas. The Kamiesberge were high granite mountains with fertile pockets, rich in birdlife and floral treasures – all the physical riches of Namaqualand were hidden there. By 1771 there were about 20 white settlers who had registered farms in Little Namaqualand.[17]

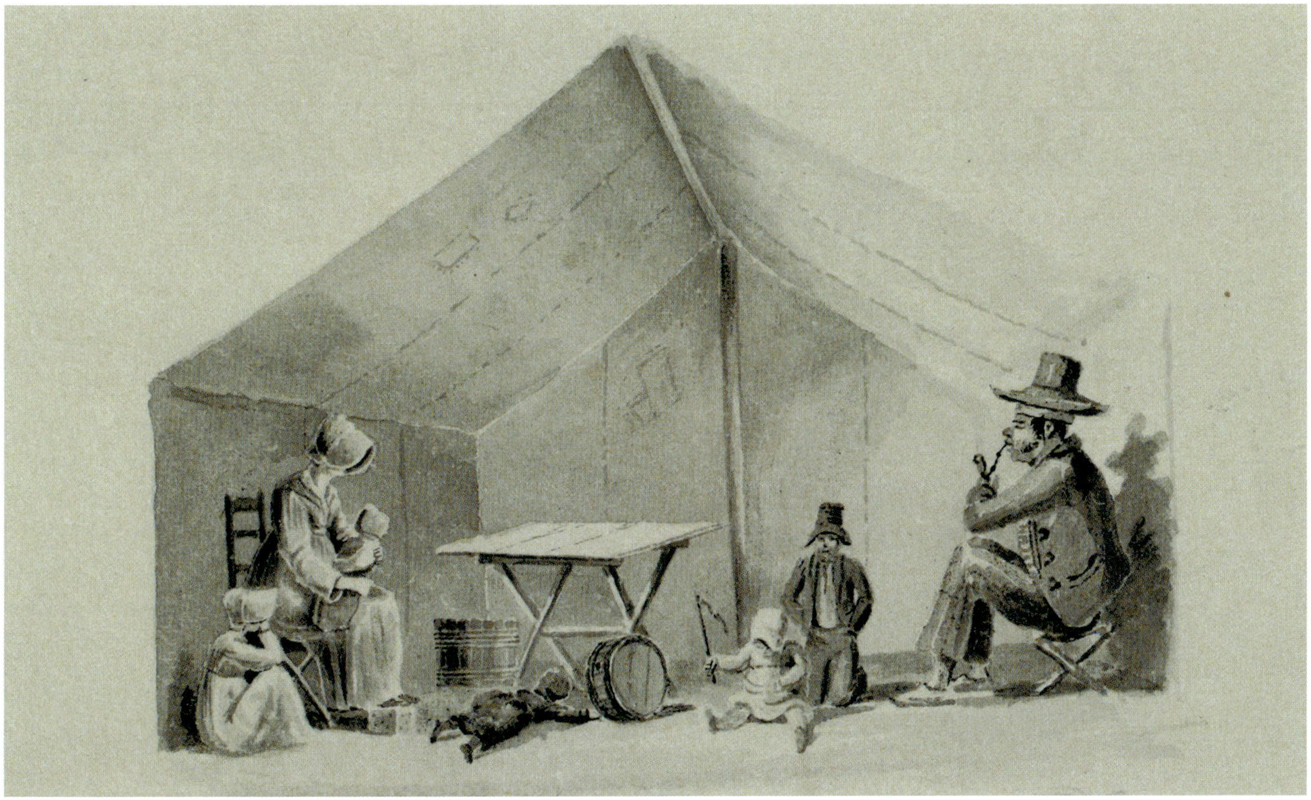

Interior of a Trekboer's tent, 1835

The *trekboers*, nomadic farmers, were frontiersmen. They lived a simple life on their grazing lands. Some camped out in their wagons, living under canvas awnings. Others, better off, built rough houses with clay walls, roofed with reeds. Hunting provided them with ivory and skins for barter on rare visits to town and a small vegetable garden produced sufficient for the household's needs. *Watercolour by Charles Davidson Bell, MuseumAfrika collection*

The missionaries were the first literate people to settle in the territory. Willem Steenkamp writes that not to mention them when telling the story of Namaqualand 'is like making bread and leaving out the yeast.'[18] They were German and English initially, armed with missionary zeal and deep religious conviction, followed by the Dutch Reformed and Roman Catholic churches.[19] Some at first trekked with the nomadic tribes. They subsequently established mission stations, such as Byzondermeid (later Steinkopf), Komaggas, Pella and Leliefontein, and became the resident missionaries for the 'Coloured' or Baster people. Leliefontein, in the Kamiesberg, was established in 1816 by the Wesleyan Missionary Institution under the Reverend Barnabas Shaw. He built a thatched mud-walled church and preached there for ten years. Pella mission station was started in 1811 by the German missionary, Christian Albrecht, under the protection of the London Missionary Society, but it was abandoned in 1825. In 1816 Rev Johann Heinrich Schmelen, a Rhenish missionary from Germany, married Khoretjie, a Coloured woman from Byzondermeid, who helped him translate the Bible into the Nama language. A Baster, Jasper Cloete, invited him to minister to the community at Komaggas and he did so from 1829 until his death in 1849.[20] Despite being criticised by later historians for creating easy labour pools for the developing copper mines, it was through the missionaries' efforts in obtaining from the government 'Tickets of Occupation'[21] that these communities secured ownership and the mission stations became Coloured reserves.[22]

In 1850 a chance discovery of copper on the quitrent farm Springbokfontein changed the face of Namaqualand forever. Springbokfontein, alias Melkboschuil, alias Koperberg, situated in the field cornetcy of Namaqualand, was owned by the descendants

Leliefontein

The Wesleyan Missionary Institution of Lily Fountain in the Kamiesberg, Little Namaqualand was established in 1816 by Rev Barnabas Shaw, an Englishman. The name 'Leliefontein' derives from the arum lilies found in the vicinity of the spring. A Namaqua, Captain Wildschut settled on the original farm in 1770.
Gogh James F, Views, etc [Paarl] 1880, Jowell collection

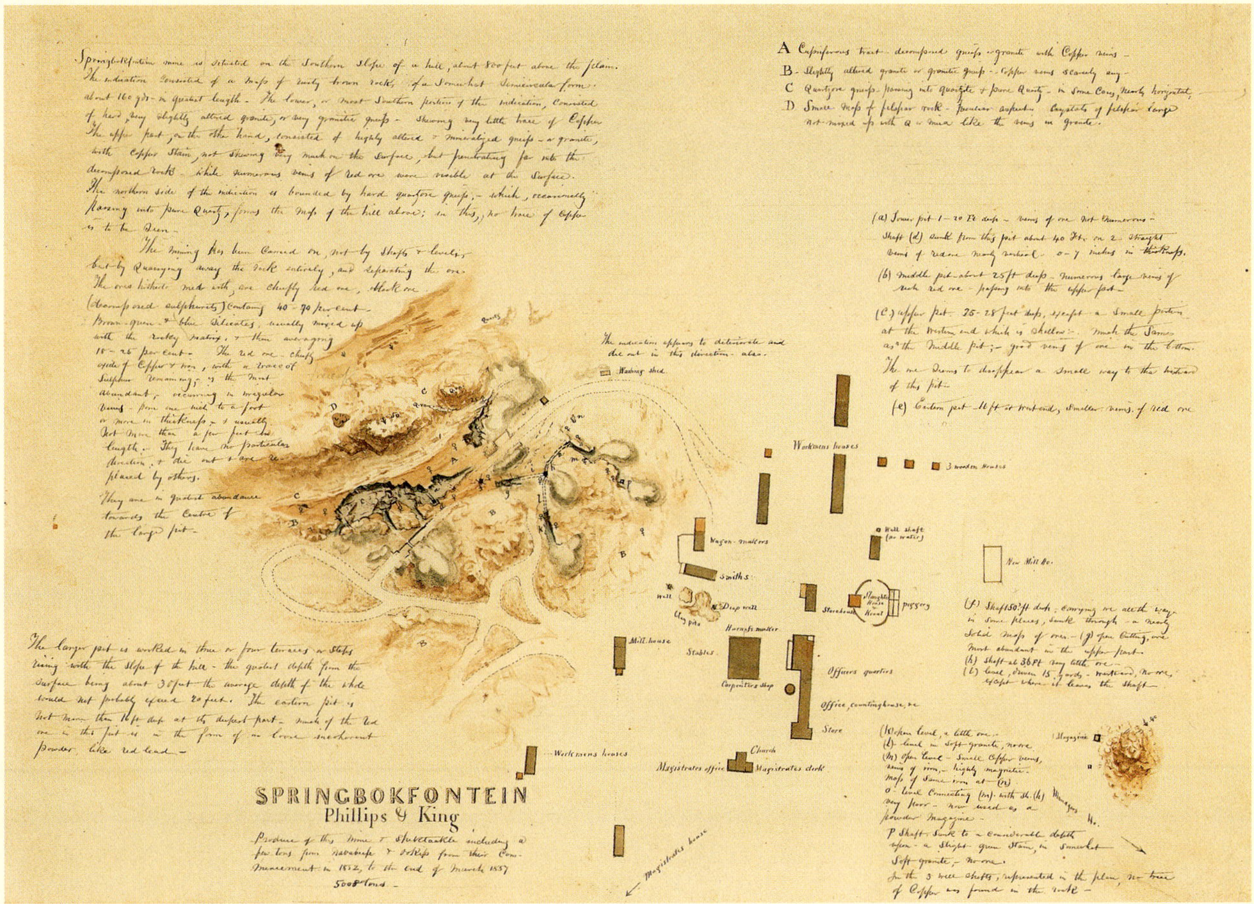

Springbokfontein, 1856

Geological sketch of Springbokfontein mine, part of the survey conducted by Andrew Wyley, Geological Surveyor to the Colony of the Cape of Good Hope, 1856. Wyley was commissioned to do a survey of the copper mines in Namaqualand in order to assess the prospects for copper mining. The drawing is interesting because it shows the earliest buildings in the mining village.

Piet Cloete, circa 1852

Piet Cloete, one of the Cloete family members who occupied the farm Springbokfontein, alias Melkboschuil, on which copper was discovered in 1850. The mineral rights to the Cloetes' farm were acquired by the company Phillips & King and this started the copper industry in Namaqualand. King's Mine, the copper mine in Springbokfontein, was the earliest commercial copper mine in South Africa.

Mendelssohn collection, Library of Parliament

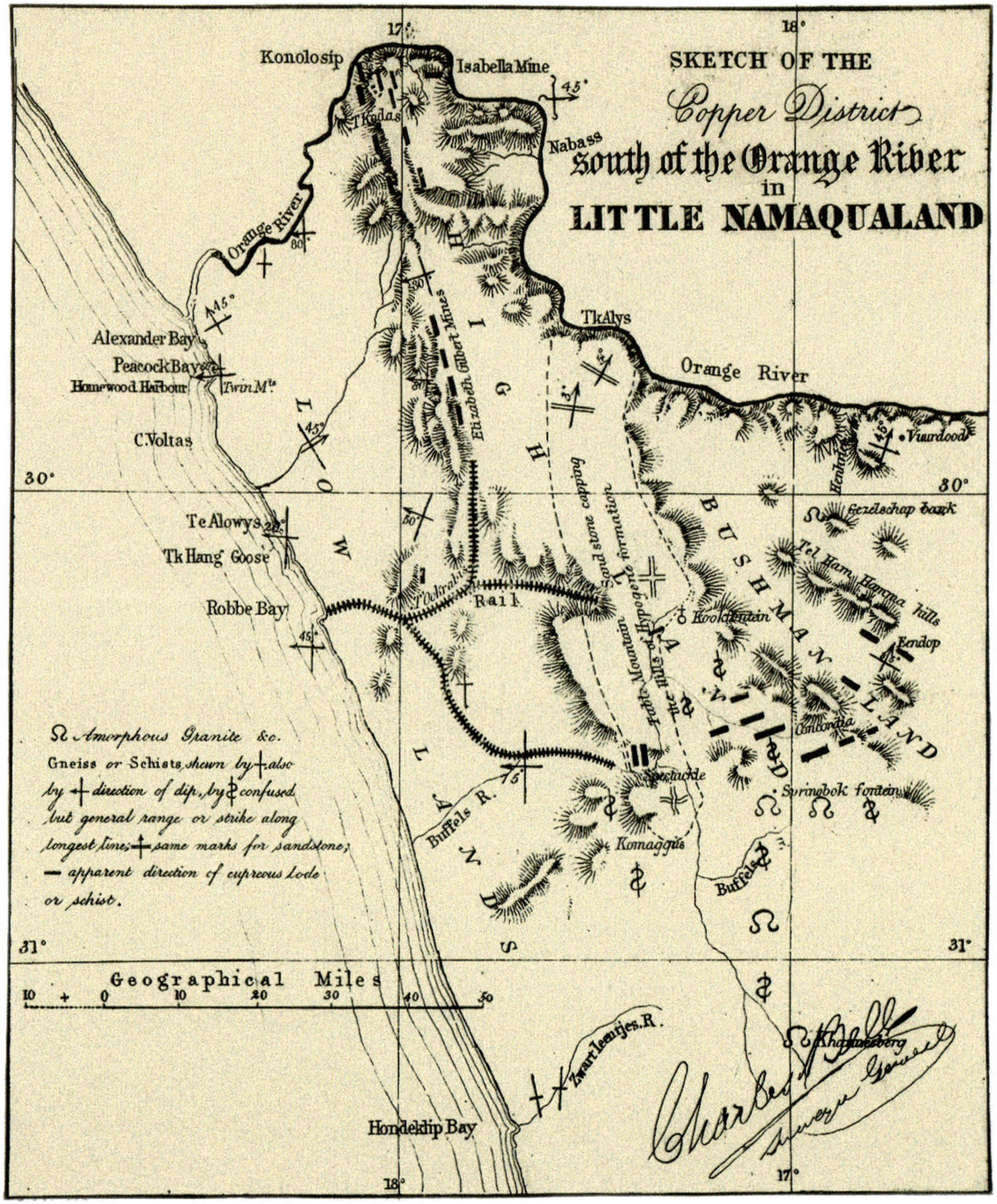

Early sketch of Little Namaqualand, 1855

Charles D Bell, Surveyor-General for the Cape of Good Hope, drew this map in 1855 of the copper district of what was called Little Namaqualand – the remote, arid and semi-desert area situated in the north-western Cape south of the Orange River (as distinct from Greater Namaqualand which is situated north of the Orange River, today known as Namibia). *Cape of Good Hope Reports of the Surveyor-General, Charles D Bell, Esq., on Copper Fields of Little Namaqualand, 1855*

Early passenger coach drawn by mules ▶

Mules pulled the first coaches on the private railway line built between Porth Nolloth and O'okiep for the transport of copper and completed in1876. The mule 'train', was generally made up of ten units (20 trucks each pulled by two mules) and a passenger 'special' (as shown in the photograph). The journey – 152 km – took two days with a welcome stop-over at Anenous after the precipitous ascent up the Anenous Pass. *Gogh album*

Anenous
Mountains

Richtersveld copper

A sizable chunk of what is termed 'native' copper found in the mountains of the Richtersveld, about 6 miles (9 km) south of Ganna Gariep, in 1918.
Betty Wright collection

of Jasper Cloete.[23] There were seven brothers, Nicholaas, Jan, Gert, Jacobus, Piet, Dirk and Jacob. The title to the farm had only just been granted to them on 21 January 1850. In March of that year the Cape Town firm of Philip & King paid them £50 for a portion of their farm and the mineral rights to the entire farm. They later purchased the remainder of the farm for £2 344 10s. Three of the brothers could sign this agreement with the purchasers, the other four made their cross.[24] The date was 13 April 1852.

Mining began in earnest in 1852 and large-scale development of copper ore followed the discovery. Springbokfontein became the first working copper mine in South Africa under the proprietorship of Phillips & King.[25] The first consignment of ore from the mine was taken overland by ox-wagon and shipped from Hondeklip Bay on 1 August 1852. This was followed by an influx of miners, prospectors, speculators and fortune-seekers. 'Copper mania' reached its height in 1854 when practically every town in the Cape Colony formed a company or syndicate of one kind or another to raise capital for the exploitation of this mineral. Springbokfontein grew into a private mining village, with quarters for workmen, offices, workshops, stores and wagonbuilders' and blacksmiths' shops.

Copper fever, however, soon subsided, the speculators left and the business of serious mining got under way. Skilled labour was imported from the Isle of Man and Cornwall. Unskilled labour was mainly obtained from the local population. The ore was transported over very rough roads to ports at Hondeklip Bay and Port Nolloth (the wagoners were mostly local farmers), but after deposits were discovered at Spectakel, Concordia, O'okiep and Nababeep, these roads were improved and later, in 1869, the construction of a railway line between O'okiep and Port Nolloth was started.

Various reports into the state of the mines and the possibilities for transport were presented to the Cape Parliament for consideration preceding the decision in 1869 to build a railway line. In 1854 A G Bain reported on the discovery of metals and the leasing of lands and Surveyor-General Charles D Bell reported on the copper fields of Little Namaqualand; Commander M S Nolloth of the H.M.S. *Frolic*, in 1855 reported on the coast south of the Orange River; and Andrew Wyley, Esq, Geological Surveyor to the Colony of the Cape of Good Hope, reported on the mineral and geological structure of South Namaqualand and the adjoining mineral districts in June 1857.

These reports provide valuable information on the area at that time. Wyley's report was accompanied by an Appendix in which he discusses drainage, soil quality, temperature, winds, springs and other waters, botanical features, animal life and 'native' population, mission stations, mining population and transport: 'This country of hills and plains … so perplexing, so difficult to comprehend … burning sun ... not a blade of grass or a drop of water … the quantity of rain that falls is exceedingly small ... but the deep sand of the valleys and river beds … acts as a preservative to the very small amount of water… the state of the roads after thunderstorms and rain … extreme heat and cold … the easterly winds … large arborescent aloes, the characteristic plants of Namaqualand … a country in which water is scarce and where animal and vegetable life is so poorly developed, is not likely to attract much population … few boers … mixed race of Bastaards … and the mining population – a miscellaneous assemblage.' [26]

In 1847 Sir Harry Smith, Governor of the Cape Colony, had extended the boundary of the Cape to the Orange River, thus including Namaqualand in the Colony. After 1856 a new division of Namaqualand was created which took care of the five mission stations and, more significantly, the copper mines. It was believed that 'this hitherto neglected division will before long become the most valuable contributor to the colony's staple export.' [27] The new division was created for fiscal purposes and not electoral – Namaqualand continued to remain under the electoral district of Clanwilliam. In 1860 Josias Rivers was appointed the first Civil Commissioner, based in Komaggas. The first meeting of the Namaqualand Divisional Council was held the following year,[28] its headquarters chosen as Springbokfontein and its main task, the building and maintaining of roads. The famous Messelpad or copper road, the improved rough wagon trail between the Springbokfontein mine and Hondeklip Bay, became the first proclaimed road by the Divisional Council. The infrastructure of Namaqualand was developing.

So, despite its reputation for harsh conditions and desert barrenness, Namaqualand was growing into a centre of mineral wealth and prosperous possibilities. With mission stations, settled farming communities, new mining villages and service centres, it is no wonder that the Jews, themselves providers of services and seekers of opportunity, were drawn here. What better place to trade and conduct business than an area where growth and development was tangible? The intrepid Aaron de Pass was the first Jew to appear on this landscape.

Messelpad

The original 'copper road' between the copper mines at O'okiep and the port at Hondeklip Bay was a rough wagon trail. It 'scrambled for 30 kilometres over precipitous brows and mountain ridges, with little or no constructed formation' (Steenkamp, p. 80). A particularly gruelling section of the road was improved, starting in 1867, under the supervision of Patrick Fletcher, the government surveyor for the district, and became known as the Messelpad (Masonry road). It still exists today – 'the Victorians made things to last' says Willem Steenkamp.
Graham Ross collection

Aaron de Pass

Aaron de Pass, the first Jewish presence in Namaqualand, was an English entrepreneur. After his arrival at the Cape in 1846, this literate, middle-class businessman made an immediate impression on commercial activities there. He was a practising Jew and became a founder member of the newly formed Jewish congregation in Cape Town. He was drawn to Namaqualand in 1851.
Cape Archives

De Pass Fleet

Aaron de Pass, and his brother Elias, became prominent in the expansion of the Cape coastal trade, which was essentially whaling and fishing. His fleet, pictured here in Durban Harbour, plied the waters from Sandwich Harbour to Mauritius.
Phoebe and Rebecca Walker collection

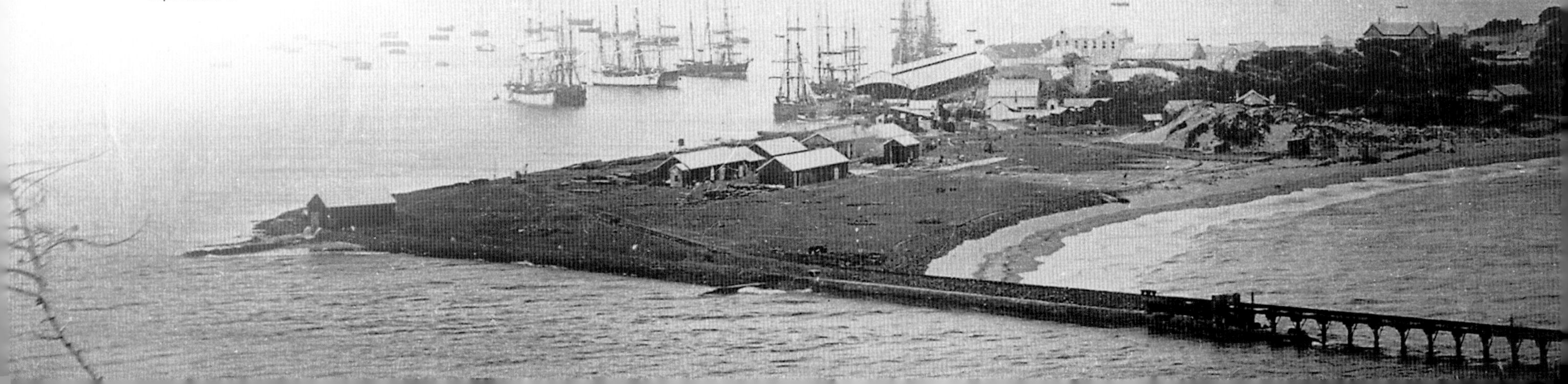

Esther de Pass

Esther de Pass, devoted wife of Aaron whom she married in 1836 aged 19, supported her husband through all his endeavours under the most extreme conditions. They made several trips to Namaqualand, sometimes lengthy, and even when so far from home and family, she remained true to her Jewish traditions.
Cape Archives

3 THE FIRST ENTREPRENEUR

Aaron de Pass, together with his younger brother, Elias, his wife, Esther, and their two children Hannah and Daniel were Sephardic Jews from London, England and arrived in South Africa in 1846. The De Pass brothers' expertise lay in the shoe and leather industry, a business they began soon after their arrival in Cape Town. But Aaron was an entrepreneur of the kind that emerged during the Industrial Revolution, and the Cape Colony offered many opportunities for his talents and interests. Within a short time of their arrival, the brothers became involved in the West Coast trade, essentially whaling and fishing. Guano, a superb fertiliser, had been discovered up the west coast near Angra Pequina, today known as Luderitz, in Namibia. The De Pass brothers (in partnership with Benjamin Norden, one of the leaders of the Jewish community in Cape Town) leased the Ichaboe and other islands, and started harvesting guano.[1] This they shipped to Mauritius and Madagascar, where sugar-cane was being farmed, together with the salted fish from fisheries they had established at Sandwich Harbour near Walvis Bay. Aaron and Elias were also responsible for building the first patent slips for shipping repairs at the Simon's Town and Cape Town harbours, which enabled ships to dock more easily.[2]

By the time copper mining sprang into life in Namaqualand, Aaron already owned a number of shipping vessels that could be used to transport copper from the port of Hondeklip Bay, at the mouth of the Olifants River. Hondeklip Bay had originally been planned as a wheat port for what was hoped would be a viable industry in Namaqualand. There was a ready market for wheat at the Cape, where drought was prevalent and the grain crops were often affected by disease.[3] Although wheat would seem to be an unlikely crop in the brackish and barren wilderness of Namaqualand, the Dutch farmers and the mission settlements as far back as 1824 were in fact growing good quality wheat. The Kamiesberg mountain region was indeed considered the 'granary of Namaqualand'[4] and was regarded as having great potential as a wheat production area if suitable land links and a convenient port for shipping the apparently abundant supplies could be established. Aaron de Pass had acquired farmland deep in the Kamiesberg mountains in 1851 in order to become involved in the wheat industry. When he gave evidence to the Parliamentary Select Committee on Namaqualand's

Wheat fields

Wheat fields in the vicinity of Steinkopf, where harvesting was done by hand. Travellers and prospectors such as George Thomson in the 1820s and Thomas Fannin in the 1840s reported glowingly on the quality of the bread they sampled on their travels. Fannin remembered the 'stewed mutton and sweet brown bread, made from wheat grown by themselves [the Dutch farmers]'. *McMillan collection, Manuscripts & Archives, UCT*

Hondeklip Bay, 1850s

Probably the earliest rendering of the port of Hondeklip Bay, in the mid 1850s. Thomas Grace established a trading station at this sheltered cove which was considered suitable for shipping wheat grown by farmers in the Kamiesberg. After copper was discovered in 1850 and mining began, the settlement was given a boost. Despite the reconstruction of the Messelpad or copper road, Phillips & King, the company that mined copper at Springbokfontein, O'okiep and Spectakel, chose in the late 1860s to use Port Nolloth rather than Hondeklip Bay as its ore port. Hondeklip Bay declined after the Government authorised the building of a railway line in 1869 and once the track from Port Nolloth reached O'okiep in 1876.
Mendelssohn collection, Library of Parliament

The Elizabeth Mary

The *Elizabeth Mary*, owned by De Pass, anchored in Walvis Bay, March 1861.
MuseumAfrika collection

Springbokfontein, 1862

Springbokfontein, in 1862, when a township was established on the copper mine property of Phillips & King.
Watercolour sketch by A W Corner
MuseumAfrika collection

Roads in 1854, he described himself as a 'landed proprietor in the Kamiesberg' who had 'carried on business in Namaqualand' for three years before that hearing.[5]

Aaron opened the first trading post in Hondeklip Bay – the first also in Namaqualand – and sent up his brother-in-law, Moses Levy Bensusan (his sister Kate's husband) to manage the establishment. Soon afterwards he opened a trading post at Port Nolloth, and also acquired mineral rights in Komaggas.

Aaron, it would appear, was not so much a 'hands on' kind of man but tended to form partnerships with those whose expertise he could rely on to run the day-to-day affairs of the ventures with which he became involved. Thus he was in partnership with John Granville Nicholson in the Hondeklip Bay store 'De Pass and Nicholson' and Captain John Spence in the shipping company 'De Pass, Spence and Co'.

Aaron, accompanied by Esther, went on three expeditions into Namaqualand, one lasting six months. They stopped over at farms and settlements, furnished with an official letter from the Colonial Office supporting their requests for assistance, accommodation and forage for their animals[6] – there were no hotels or inns on the road, but, according to reports, the Dutch farmers were friendly and hospitable.[7] They also visited Komaggas and Spectakel where copper was being mined and set up home for a while in Hondeklip Bay.

Esther must have been a remarkable woman. She was only nineteen years of age when she married Aaron in England and accompanied him wherever he went in the world. Anyone who has spent a summer in Namaqualand knows of the heat and dust that make life unbearable. There were few creature comforts for travellers in those days and what with the fashion of the day, travel for Esther must have been most uncomfortable. Where did she wash? Did they carry their own water supplies? We have no way of knowing the answers, but admire her for her stoicism. She heralded an era of strong women who accompanied or joined their husbands in Namaqualand during the ensuing one hundred years and supported them in their endeavours.

Esther and Aaron were practising Jews. Aaron had been involved in the purchase of the new synagogue in Cape Town in 1849, the first in South Africa, and had become its first *Parnas* (synagogue dignitary).[8] The story of how Aaron and Esther observed *Yom Kippur* in Port Nolloth has already been told.

Production at the copper mine at Springbokfontein had started declining and had dropped from 2 100 tons of ore in 1857 to 437 tons in 1861, so Phillips & King decided to start disposing of its property. The company made plans to sell off part of the farm Melkboschuil and lay out a public village in Springbokfontein. In 1911 its name was officially changed to Springbok. Patrick Fletcher, the surveyor, himself a resident of Namaqualand, was given the task and in 1862 44 erven were sold – the chief landowner being the Cape Copper Company.

Raphael Bensusan, another of Aaron's brothers-in-law, was among the first to purchase land. He became the owner of erven 77 and 78. Part of his motivation may have been the promise of preferential contracts to transport copper from O'okiep to Hondeklip Bay for purchasers of plots. What he was doing in Namaqualand is not recorded, although the serious depression at the Cape in the 1860s may have brought him there to join the family ventures. All in all, Raphael spent ten years in Namaqualand – he seems to have been involved in guns and ammunition dealings over the Orange River. He ended up in Kimberley when diamonds were discovered there in 1870.

Aaron eventually returned to England in 1869. He was only 54 years old, but was already worn out by his enormous drive, energy and enterprise. As he wrote in his Journal 'my health not good from overwork (sic) of the brain and heart'.[9] He died in 1877. Although none of the De Pass or Bensusan families ever settled in Namaqualand, and although not typical of the Jews that followed some years later, they did establish the first trading posts in the area. Their brief tenure also revealed the trends of kinship, family networking and observance of Jewish faith, which would become distinct markers of Jewish life in Namaqualand.

Spectakel mine

Spectakel mine circa 1880. Phillips & King obtained a lease to work this site in 1853 and it looked for a time as if the mine would be highly productive. In fact, for a brief spell, Spectakel was the largest village in Namaqualand. After successive stoppages and failures, mining activity had virtually ceased by 1908/9. *Gogh album*

4 SUGAR, SOAP AND VELSKOENE

The next Jew after Aaron de Pass to appear on the local scene, according to our records, was Moses Schur, a Lithuanian immigrant from Chaviadan. His era in Namaqualand spanned the years 1881 – 1915. His is really the more typical story. He started off as a *smous*, an itinerant trader. These early Jewish *smouse* from Lithuania spoke Yiddish which had some similarities with the Dutch spoken by the farmers at that time, so they were able to communicate fairly easily by fusing the two languages.[1] The following examples: *handlen* (to do business), *mekler* (agent or salesman) and *baroof* (occupation or career) have similar roots in Afrikaans and Yiddish.[2] The *smouse* travelled from farm to farm bringing wares and news. They called on the mission stations, Leliefontein, Steinkopf, Pella and Komaggas and the copper mines of Springbokfontein, O'okiep, Nababeep, Concordia and Spectakel.[3]

Life was hard for the *smous*. He had to slog on foot. He was often forced to sleep in the open *veld* (countryside) and was exposed to the dangers of attack by man and wild animals (there were leopards in Namaqualand). The weight of his pack might well exceed 80 lbs (36 kg) – he carried articles such as material, needles, cotton thread, thimbles, buttons, hooks and eyes and also matches, tobacco, pipes, knives, jewellery and Dutch medicines. But he was prepared to work hard and suffer privations in order to improve his position. The hospitality of the Namaqualand farming families helped ease his situation somewhat – he was given accommodation and food, his clothes were washed and his *velskoene* (home-made shoes) repaired. The *smous* in return brought gifts for the farmer, a penknife or pipe, and an attractive piece of fabric or a brooch for his wife.[4] The *smous* was a welcome guest in these isolated parts.

Moses Schur & family

Moses Schur, who hailed from Chaviadan in Lithuania, was the first Jewish shopkeeper to establish himself in Namaqualand. He started off as a *smous* and soon had several stores in the area, which his sons managed. He is pictured here with his second wife, Leah, and two of their children, Samuel and Sophie. Two sons from his first marriage, Philip & Louis, are standing behind him.
Milton Simanowitz collection

It is said that the first time Moses Schur appeared in Namaqualand he was on foot carrying a pack on his back; the next time the pack was on a donkey; the following year both Schur and pack were on a cart drawn by two donkeys and the year after that Schur opened a shop in the little village of Bowesdorp – the pattern for so many *smouse*. The donkey was originally imported in 1656 from the Cape Verde Islands to provide transport for grain farmers in the Malmesbury district. They made their appearance in Namaqualand as draught and transport animals as early as the mid-1800s. The first railway in Namaqualand, which ran between the copper mines at O'okiep and the port at Port Nolloth from 1876, was in fact mule-powered. Mules, a cross between a mare and a male donkey, were hardy little animals well

◀ Josman Store, O'okiep

Interior of Louis Josman's store in O'okiep circa 1915. Louis Josman (right) was always immaculately groomed in photographs taken of him and the interior of this store reflects the same attention to detail and meticulous care. As a general dealer and tailor, he had stores in both O'okiep and Garies, a butchery and a farm near Garies. He was in Namaqualand between 1906 and 1945. Four children were born to him and Dora (Dolly), two of them in Garies. In this photograph, Louis Nainkin, who assisted in the store and butchery, appears with him.
Sonny Josman collection

Hawker's Credit Book

A page from a Hawker's Credit Book October, 1916, showing the trade in skins. Skins were regularly traded or bought by the hawkers. After copper, wool and skins were the second most important exports from the Cape Colony during the latter half of the nineteenth century.

Goats – the skin trade

The Namaqua were observed to be herding goats as early as the seventeenth century and although at times they kept sheep, today, in the twenty-first century, goats have replaced sheep as the main subsistence of poor Namaqua.
Cape Archives

Inventory of *smous* cart ▶

An inventory taken of the Cape cart of a *smous*, Abraham Jowell, gives a good idea of the type of goods carried by such *smouse*. They included items such as haberdashery, scales, spectacles, combs, silver watches, gold rings, cufflinks, collar studs, cutlery, flutes, clothing and linen.

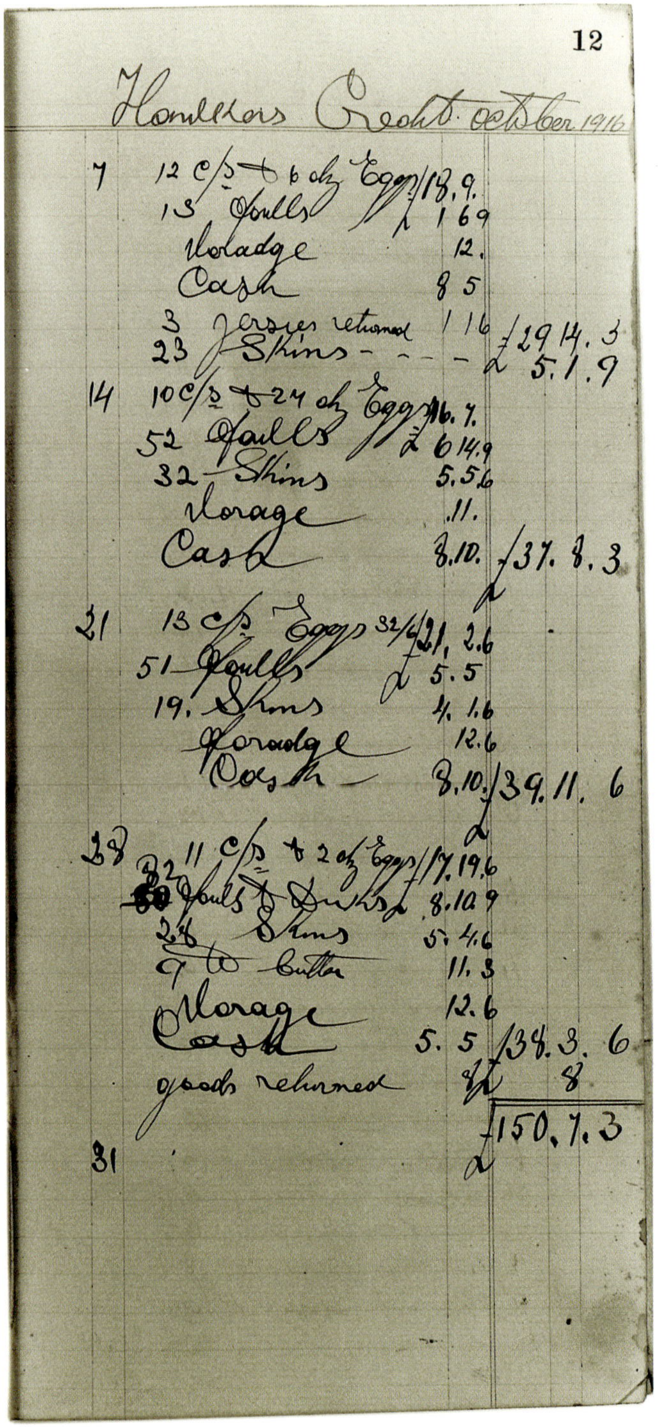

12

Hawkers Credit October 1916

7 12 c/s + 6 doz Eggs 18.9.
13 Fowls £1 6 9
Voradge 12.
Cash 8 5
3 Jerseys returned 1 16 £29 14. 3
23 Skins £5. 1. 9
14 10 c/s + 24 doz Eggs 16. 7.
52 Fowls £6 14. 9
32 Skins 5. 5. 6
Vorage .11.
Cash 8. 10. £37. 8. 3
21 13 c/s Eggs 32/6 21. 2. 6
51 Fowls £5. 5
19. Skins 4. 1. 6
Voradge 12. 6
Cash 8. 10. £39. 11. 6
28 11 c/s + 2 doz Eggs 17. 19. 6
32 Fowls & Ducks 8. 10 9
24 Skins 5. 4. 6
9 lb butter 11. 3
Vorage 12. 6
Cash 5. 5 £38. 3. 6
goods returned 8
£150. 7. 3
31

suited to Namaqualand conditions.

Moses Schur is mentioned in the reminiscences of the young *Dominee* (Minister) of the Dutch Reformed Church, Ds W J Conradie. In 1895 he was conducting a pastoral tour of his parish of Namaqualand, established forty-five years earlier. Bowesdorp was by then the spiritual centre for this community and had a fine stone church and a school with boarding facilities. Conradie refers to '*die hier een bloeiende bezigheid drift*'[5] and relates that Schur offered him delicacies such as atjar, sardines and salmon, asking nothing in return except that the *Dominee* pray for his family – '*Bid ver ons en ons moet ver meneer sorre*'.[6] Here again we encounter another devout Jew, one who is both generous and responsive to a religious leader of another faith. Schur is reputed to have travelled with a *schochet* (ritual slaughterer) between Bowesdorp and Cape Town, where he later established a home, and is said to have prayed each morning on waking.

Schur's two Jewish assistants, Mr A Schneider and Mr A Berman, were also observant Jews – they acted as *wagters* after Abraham Jowell, a *smous*, had a fatal accident with his mule cart in the Kamiesberge in 1898. They sat with the body at the farm Olienfontein until the burial there in the Van Niekerk's family cemetery.

They did not, however, travel to Springbokfontein to attend the inquest a few days later as 'it was the Sabbath'.[7] Evidence at the inquest was provided by Abraham Jowell's Coloured assistant, Jan Fortuin, who told the magistrate that the cart, drawn by four mules, was carrying something like 1500 lbs (675 kg).

Moses Schur was an industrious and enterprising man and recognised the trading opportunities that existed in Namaqualand. There were the new mining towns to be serviced – O'okiep, the headquarters of the Cape Copper Company, Nababeep and Springbok.[8] He established himself throughout the district in a short time and appointed his sons, Joseph, Woolf and Harry to manage the various stores. Joseph also travelled around Namaqualand buying skins – a viable commodity in South Africa at the time.

Livestock was, of course, an intrinsic part of Namaqualand's history – the name Namaqualand means *die land van die karos of veldraer*.[9] The Khoi people had migrated to the area much earlier with their flocks, and Simon van der Stel had observed the Namaqua herding oxen, sheep and goats and carrying copper in skin knapsacks.[10] The frontier farmers or *trekboers* also kept livestock and used skin for clothing and coverings (known as *karosses*). Livestock traders bartered skins with the Khoikhoi and *trekboers* so that by the time the early *toggers* or *smouse* reached Namaqualand there was already a practise of dealing in skins. In fact, James Roux, a fifth-generation farmer in Namaqualand, relates that his maternal grandparents, the Kennedys, smoused inland after they arrived by boat at Hondeklip Bay from Scotland in the 1850s. From the late 1800s the Jewish *smouse* became the middlemen in the lucrative skin trade – skins from sheep and goats were second only to wool in being the chief exports from the Cape Colony in 1874. By 1904 the number of skins emanating from Namaqualand had reached a total of 36 434.[11]

When Moses died in Cape Town in 1915, he owned a number of stores in the main mining towns (either run

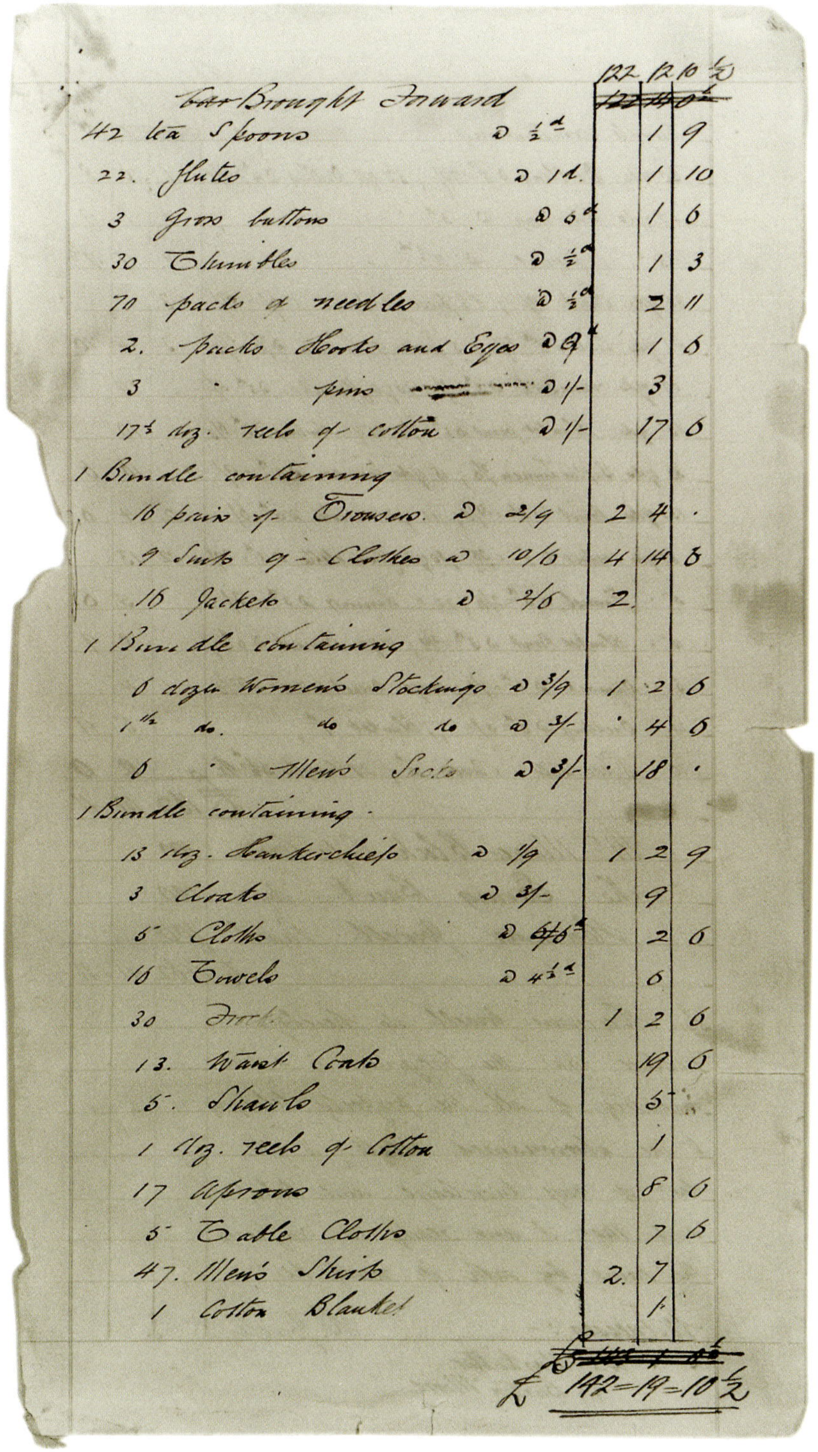

		£	s	d
Brought Forward		122	12	10½
42 tea Spoons	@ ½d		1	9
22. flutes	@ 1d.		1	10
3 gross buttons	@ 6d		1	6
30 Thimbles	@ ½d		1	3
70 packs of needles	@ ½d		2	11
2. packs Hooks and Eyes	@ 9d		1	6
3 pins	@ 1/-		3	
17½ doz. reels of cotton	@ 1/-		17	6
1 Bundle containing				
16 pair of Trousers	@ 2/9	2	4	.
9 Suits of Clothes	@ 10/6	4	14	6
16 Jackets	@ 2/6	2		
1 Bundle containing				
6 dozn Women's Stockings	@ 3/9	1	2	6
1½ do. do do	@ 3/-	.	4	6
6 Men's Socks	@ 3/-	.	18	.
1 Bundle containing				
15 doz. Handkerchiefs	@ 1/9	1	2	9
3 Coats	@ 3/-		9	
6 Cloths	@ [illegible]		2	6
16 Towels	@ 4½d		6	
30 Frocks		1	2	6
13. Waist Coats			19	6
5. Shawls			5	
1 doz. reels of cotton			1	
17 Aprons			8	6
5 Table Cloths			7	6
47. Men's Shirts		2	7	
1 Cotton Blanket			1	
£		142	19	10½

Street scene in Garies

The main street in Garies with a view of the Garies Hotel. This is a really swinging town!
The shop and hotel were run from the 1890s by Maurice Eilenberg's brother-in-law, Philip Rosenberg, together with his wife Minnie. This photo shows the simple environment in which Jewish immigrants established themselves.
Rosenberg family collection

Maurice & Hannah Eilenberg

Maurice Eilenberg was an early shopkeeper in Garies. Here he and his wife Hannah, who is wearing a motoring veil against the dust, are setting off from Cape Town to open the new Garies public library in 1910. His arrival in Garies must have caused a sensation – apparently the locals ran away at the sight of this strange animal!
Rosenberg family collection

by his sons or leased out), business premises on a farm, two farms and homes in Bowesdorp and Cape Town. His extraordinary business ability had enabled him to develop from a humble *smous* in 1881, to a greatly admired businessman 30 years later; his firm, M Schur & Sons, being synonymous with business in Namaqualand.

At the same time as Moses Schur was starting up in Bowesdorp, Maurice Eilenberg was making his way to Namaqualand. Interestingly, here too, it is Dutch Reformed Church records that provide evidence of when he first appeared on the local scene. In a history of Garies, it is mentioned that the first post office was built in 1887 but that prior to that year, 'Meester Eilenberg' provided the postal services for the village. Early Jewish historians record him as having opened a store in Garies in the late 1870s.[12]

Garies was in a strategic position. It was the centre for church activities, preferred to Bowesdorp by the young *Dominee* Conradie for his '*uitgestrekte gemeenskap*';[13] it was the centre for good farming, lying at the foot of the Kamiesberg mountains which, as we have seen, was the main watering place for the indigenous peoples of Namaqualand; and it was on the route to the Western Cape. The town's history dates back to the early *trekboers* who settled in the Kamiesberge in 1780. In 1844 a farmer, Hermanus Rossouw, laid out a village on his farm Goedverwachting and donated ground to the Dutch Reformed Church. It was around this *kerkplek* that the little town started to grow and its growth went hand in hand with the expansion of church activity. The advertisements for the sale of plots in 1884 spoke of '*die meest vruchtbare en productieve in het District … gelykstaande in opbrengst met die beste eigendom te Wynberg en Rondebosch*'[14] but this wasn't quite so! Householders still had to catch the *dakwatertjies* and use sparingly![15]

Maurice Eilenberg came from Krakow, Austria, (today Poland). He married Hannah Rosenberg who had come out from Germany as governess to the children of a Jewish family in Cape Town. He also brought out her entire family and set up her brother, Philip, in Namaqualand to run the shop and hotel in Garies. There is no evidence that Maurice and Hannah lived in Garies after their marriage, but he remained committed to the town's welfare.

Philip Rosenberg married Minnie Barnett in 1894 and together they ran the Garies Hotel with a shop attached that they had taken over from Maurice Eilenberg. They spent many years there and their son Max Harry was born in Garies in 1897.

Henry Barnett owned a general dealer's store called H Barnett & Co also referred to in Dutch Reformed Church records. Henry was married to Hannah Eilenberg's sister, Helena. These two Garies stores were favourably mentioned in a history of the church in that area: '*dan hebben we hier nog twee winkels waar men van alles sowat kan krijgen.*'[16]

The theme of Jewish kinship and family networking continues with the appearance on the local scene of Joseph Dembitzer. He was a close relative of Maurice Eilenberg from Krakow and came from a large family. He was ambitious and wanted to make his way in life so in 1890, Eilenberg brought him out as well, and set him up in business in Springbokfontein after he had smoused in the area for a while. The Dembitzer Store was the first Jewish business in that town and after Joseph married Pollie Barnett (Minnie Rosenberg's niece) she became the first Jewish woman in Springbokfontein. There was only a handful of other women living there at the time, mostly wives of Cape Copper Company officials.

Joseph Dembitzer expanded his business and brought out his brothers Simon and Joel to help him. He also employed Isaac Friedlander in 1899 who had recently arrived from Latvia and been recommended to him as a shop assistant. Later, Isaac Friedlander, like many other shop assistants, branched out independently and started his own shop. By the time Joseph retired to Cape Town in 1916, he had stores in Springbokfontein, O'okiep and Nababeep and a hotel in

Three brothers-in-law

Philip Rosenberg, Maurice Eilenberg and Henry Barnett (l. to r), three brothers-in-law with business interests in Garies.
Rosenberg family collection

die meest vruchtbare … : 'the most fruitful and productive in the district … comparable with the best properties in Wynberg and Rondebosch'

dan hebben we … : 'Then there are two shops where one can get everything.'

Schapera and Josephson , Bowesdorp

Max Schapera and Solomon Josephson outside their store in Bowesdorp. In 1921 they entered into a partnership and took over the business of M Schur & Son. Abe Schapera, Max's brother, joined them in the business that same year.
Raphael Schapera collection

Teen die end ... : 'Towards the end of the previous [nineteenth] century, every little town had its few Jewish shops, dependent on the size of the community, even on some large farms, such as Gamoep, Grootvlei, Namies, Wallekraal and Grootmist, there were shops.'

As kind was... : 'As a child, it was always a treat to visit a Jewish shop because, while your parents did business, the owner would press a few sweets into your hand. Most shops had a similar set-up: a long counter along the middle, on the counter a row of glass bottles with assorted sweets ... On the shelves behind the counter, all the groceries, on the left, fabrics, and on the right, medicines. Above, from the roof hung a variety of goods – rope, bicycle wheels, handmade skin shoes, paraffin lamps, scarves in every colour. In front of the counter stood half-opened bags of sugar, flour, beans, coffee beans and green peas. The shopkeeper would wrap purchases of loose sugar or tea in pieces of newspaper twisted into packets.'

the coastal port of Port Nolloth.

When Herman Schapera came from Belorussia in 1898, he joined Moses Schur in his store in Nababeep but soon started his own in Garies. With the large farming community and the mother church of the Dutch Reformed Church having relocated there some years earlier, there was enough business for three stores. He was married when he came to Namaqualand and three years later his wife produced a son, whom they named Max. Years later, after matriculating at Paarl Boys Gymnasium, Max would return to Namaqualand and buy up all the Schur stores and properties.

By the end of the century there was a Jew in every *dorp* (village). Theunis Uys writes:

> Teen die end van die vorige eeue het elke dorpie sy paar jodewinkels gehad, afhangende van die grootte van die gemeenskap, op party groot plase was daar selfs winkels soos Gamoep, Grootvlei, Namies, Wallekraal en Grootmist.[17]

As a child, Theunis loved the Jewish shops. He describes their interior, particularly the sweets:

> As kind was dit altyd 'n plesier om in a jodewinkel te kom want as jou ouers 'n besigheidjie gedoen het, maak nie saak hoe gering dan het die winkelbaas altyd die kinders 'n paar hotnotsklontlekkers in die hand gestop. Alle winkels het min of meer dieselfde patron gehad. 'n Lang toonbank in die middle af. Op die toonbank was 'n ry glasbottels met lekkergoed, borssuikers, hotnotsklontjies, niggerbols, geselskaplekkers of vrylekkers soos ons hulle ook genoem het. In die rakke agter die toonbank was alle kruideniersware, in die rakke links was al die materiale en aan die regtekant was die medisyne. Bo in die dak reg bokant die toonbank het 'n groot verskeidenheid van goed gehang, tuie, fietswiele, velskoene, kastrole lanterns en kopdoeke in al water 'n kleur is. Voor die toonbank het halfoop sakke gestaan met suiker, miel, boontjies, koffiepitte, stampmielies en ertjies. As jy losgoed soos suiker of tee koop het die winkelbaas somar van 'n stuk koerant papier 'n kardoes gedraai en dit daarin gegooi.[18]

These first Jewish immigrants pioneered the entrepreneurial shopkeeping spirit which was to thrive for years to come. They started with little or no capital, soon set up country stores and introduced the beginnings of a money-exchange system. The role of the immigrant storekeeper and produce dealer in gathering, distributing and financing marketable produce would transform the economy of Namaqualand from a currency based on sheep and goats to one based on money. The society was brought into the twentieth century and the Jews grew from simple itinerant pedlars and shopkeepers into successful business achievers.[19]

Gradually the immigrants were putting down roots in their new country. A first generation of South Africans was being born who would continue their parents' work. Village life was developing which would leave an indelible mark on this new generation of Jewish South Africans, but not before the Anglo-Boer War had interrupted the flow of life in these little country towns.

Dembitzer home

Joseph Dembitzer married Pollie Barnett and this photo shows her and three of her sons in front of their family home in Springbokfontein. Pollie was the first Jewish woman there and gave birth to all four of her children in Springbokfontein. Notice the pepper trees outside the home. Planting of these was an activity of the schoolboys, to provide shade for this semi-desert town.
Max Dembitzer collection

J. Dembitzer, businessman

Joseph Dembitzer had stores in Springbokfontein, O'okiep and Nababeep and a hotel, the Commercial Hotel, in Port Nolloth. His brothers, Simon and Joel, assisted him. Joseph is pictured here with two of his sons, Harry and Mannie.
Max Dembitzer collection

The 'good-for' coin could be exchanged for goods in the shop.

Max Dembitzer collection

Dembitzer shop, Springbokfontein, 1895

Before he was married, Joseph Dembitzer lived in this simple house attached to his shop in Springbokfontein.
Max Dembitzer collection

Springbokfontein in the 1880s

The town of Springbokfontein has always had its ups and downs. After high-quality copper ore was discovered in O'okiep, a few kilometres away, the centre of mining activity moved there and the mining personnel moved across. Although the town became practically deserted the magistracy remained, and when the mine was reopened in 1881 after shipping costs dropped, life returned. When W C Scully arrived as magistrate in 1886, he found an attractive village of 200 inhabitants. Shortly afterwards the Divisional Council of Namaqualand was established there and the town's population reflected life in a public village with shops, a hotel, a church and a jail! Mining continued sporadically at the Springbokfontein mine but finally came to an end in 1892.
Gogh album

5 COMMANDEERED INTO WAR

The Anglo-Boer War, the 'biggest ever small war of late Victorian Imperialism',[1] impacted on world history and touched the remote region of Namaqualand as well. The war, which began in 1899, was between Great Britain on the one hand, and the independent Boer republics of the Transvaal and the Orange Free State on the other. The reasons for the war are complex and include political and strategic factors, but the main cause was undoubtedly economic.

Gold had been discovered on the Transvaal highveld in 1886, and by the mid-1890s the Witwatersrand had become the world's largest producer of gold. Britain, as the dominant economic power in the world, with London the world's financial capital, saw it as essential that the gold mines were developed efficiently. The Transvaal government under Paul Kruger believed its independence to be under threat from the combined efforts of the mine-owners, several of whom had been involved in the abortive Jameson Raid of December 1895 to overthrow the Transvaal government, and the British imperialists demanding political reforms. So, together with the Orange Free State, the Transvaal government declared war on Britain in October 1899.

The British expected the war to be over in a few months but the Boers scored a number of military successes. However, after the major Boer defeat at Paardeberg in February 1900, and the capture of the Republican capitals of Bloemfontein and Pretoria by June 1900, the Boer commandos resorted to guerrilla warfare to disrupt supply lines and prevent the consolidation of British military power. A diversionary strategy was devised to draw the Boers of the Cape Colony into the war and to force the British troops into this remote region. Jan Christiaan Smuts, then Assistant Commandant-General (and only 27 years of age), was instructed to direct an invasion into Namaqualand in September 1901.

It is difficult to imagine why anyone would have an interest in that 'arid and desolate'[2] region, but in fact the British garrison was very strong in Namaqualand. The troops were there to protect the valuable copper mines, the Port Nolloth to O'okiep railway and the Port Nolloth harbour owned by the Cape Copper Company of London. A strong British force under Major W S Shelton had been stationed in the area since January 1901, and for the last eighteen months of the war, until May 1902, British garrisons defended Namaqualand. Shelton's job was to protect 17 500 square miles (45 325 km²) of territory with a population of only 17 000 from Boer infiltration – Smuts had 1 200 troops under his command.

It is well documented by South African Jewish

Welcoming the troops

The British garrison defended the important copper mining towns of O'okiep, Concordia and Nababeep, the Port Nolloth to O'okiep railway and the Port Nolloth harbour owned by the Cape Copper Company of London. Here the locals from Port Nolloth are seen welcoming the British troops.
Tudor collection, Manuscripts & Archives, UCT

◀ General Smuts and the Boers

General Jan C Smuts led the Boer commando into Namaqualand, an incursion which ended with the Siege of O'okiep and heralded the end of the Anglo-Boer War in 1902. The Boers' sortie into the Cape was a strategy devised by Smuts to draw recruits for the depleted forces and to cause a tactical diversion from the Transvaal and the Orange Free State.
Cape Archives

Nautilus

The little boats that plied up and down the west coast between Cape Town and Port Nolloth brought goods and passengers. The trip was often very rough. The *Nautilus* was one of the best known of the Cape coasters, owned by Smith Webster, a Cape Town firm with a store in Port Nolloth. The vessel was specifically ordered for this service and replaced Berry's *Namaqua* which was wrecked in 1889. She carried about 20 saloon passengers and 'practically everyone who had anything to do with the opening up of the west coast travelled, at one time or another, in the *Nautilus*'. Many of the Jews came that route. The *Nautilus* was utilised during the Anglo-Boer War to convey stores between Cape Town and Port Nolloth. She was wrecked in 1919. (Murray, *Ships and SA*, p.256) *Robert and Bella Silverman family collection from an original owned by Peter D Faure*

Paul Kahn

Paul Kahn, newly arrived in South Africa, was commandeered by the British in Namaqualand.
Kahn family collection

scholars today that Jews fought on both sides of the Anglo-Boer War. David Saks, historian with the South African Jewish Board of Deputies, estimates that there were 300 on the Boer side (250 in the commandos and 50 in a reserve capacity such as town guards). However, there were nearly 3 000 Jews in the Imperial forces (the majority, of course, being regulars or volunteers who came out with the forces from England).[3] All burgers (citizens) were conscripted and those Jews who had citizenship rights were commandeered along with everyone else. Town guards were formed.[4] The Namaqualand Town Guards comprised 206 white miners and 661 Coloureds, all untrained. The Namaqualand Border Scouts was also formed – local men who knew the area well. Blockhouses were built by the British to provide defence of all strategic points.

Of course there were not many Jews in Namaqualand at that time but those that were, soon became involved in the war. Paul Kahn had not been in the country long enough to be conscripted but nevertheless he was commandeered by the British. He was new to the area when war broke out on 11 October 1899. He had come penniless from Klein Bechstein in Courland, Latvia and started as a *smous* in the Garies area, going from farm to farm, and had soon improved his position sufficiently to buy a wagon and a team of mules. Before he even had time to buy his first load of merchandise he 'ran into a British patrol', his daughters told. He was put into uniform and with his own wagon and mules became a transport rider for the British for the duration of the war.

Martial law was proclaimed throughout the district

Dembitzer store

This picture shows the end of the railway line at O'okiep with Dembitzer's store ahead. c. 1902
Tudor collection, Manuscripts & Archives, UCT

and nobody was allowed to travel without a pass signed by the military Commandant or his deputies. All exports and imports of goods, particularly ammunition, were restricted to prevent the Boers hijacking supplies. Joseph Dembitzer, for instance, required a government contract for supplies for his stores in Springbokfontein and O'okiep.[5] Dynamite was sold by the storekeepers for blasting in the mines, but in Boer hands it became a novel and lethal weapon used to make dynamite hand grenades to destroy the blockhouses. Other Jewish shopkeepers similarly affected were Philip Rosenberg, Herman Schapera, P Kaplan and the Schurs.[6]

The British received their mail and supplies via the railway line at Piketberg Road and then by post cart to O'okiep. Supply ships such as the SS *Nautilus* also brought additional supplies and mail to the garrison and field force via Port Nolloth. The British garrison kept wheat, meat (of which there was a plentiful supply) and flour in the food stores of the Garrison Headquarters.[7]

The Boers, organized into small commando units, invaded the area on four different fronts and recruited local Boer volunteers (labelled 'rebel' troops by the British). Quite a few came from Garies – had they been taken prisoner by the British, they would have been shot.[8] They galloped around the countryside sniping at the British whenever they could.

The Boers looted the traders' stores. Each commando unit had to forage for itself and obtain supplies of ammunition, food and clothing from the land. Stories of looting were heard from shopkeepers all over

Mule train

The 91 1/2 mile-long (146 km) railway line from O'okiep to Port Nolloth was a narrow-gauge railway drawn by mules. This picture shows the mule train, fully laden with troops, setting off for O'okiep in a typical Port Nolloth fog. *Tudor collection, Manuscripts and Archives, UCT*

Namaqualand. Philip Rosenberg in Garies reported the loss of boots and clothing valued at £214 14s; Herman Schapera's store suffered damage because the Boers pulled up the floors in his shop and took provisions valued at £14 18s; food, clothing and horses were taken from Schur's shop in Bowesdorp; Max Abel's store in Doornkraal was looted to the value of £70. For all these articles commandeered, the Boers left signed notes or receipts.

No one was allowed to trade with the Boers but Joseph Schur in Bowesdorp did so anyway. He was fined £500 (a large sum in those days), but said he'd be a fool not to as the Boers paid him for their purchases whereas the British only offered compensation for goods forcibly taken by the raiders. The British had also instructed him to burn down his stores in the event of the enemy approaching Bowesdorp.

Colonel Shelton's order to stop all foodstuffs being imported into Namaqualand was followed by a similar regulation to check the export of food into German South-West Africa via Ramans Drift and Schuit Drift. Shelton reported in a communication to Cape Town in November 1901, that 'the enemy has been unusually active all along the Orange River' and convoys of supplies were being attacked and captured. One such wagon, fully loaded with supplies, as well as 86 head of

O'okiep mine

During the Anglo-Boer War the Boers besieged O'okiep for a month, but the mine, owned by the Cape Copper Company of London was defended by the British garrison under Colonel Shelton and suffered no damage.
Above: Washing machinery at the mine.
Gogh album
Below: Miners preparing to go underground with candles attached to their helmets.
H.R. Moffatt collection, National Library of South Africa, Cape Town

cattle, was captured by the Boers between O'okiep and Pella. The further restrictions on trade caused much hardship for the traders, who were keen to transact business on both sides of the river.

The Boers advanced towards O'okiep passing through Leliefontein, Garies, Rietkloof, Bowesdorp and Mesklip. Their assault on the important mining areas of Springbokfontein, O'okiep and Concordia began at the end of March 1902. These towns were all held by mixed garrisons of British troops and Coloured levies. Smuts and his 300 men first moved on Springbokfontein and used dynamite hand grenades to disable the three blockhouses. The town surrendered after 17 hours of fighting and prisoners were held captive at the Loynes Hotel. Joseph Dembitzer's store was opened and rifled, and his naturalisation papers, issued to him in 1893/4, were stolen.[9]

Concordia came next and fell without firing a single shot so that a large quantity of dynamite, rifles and rounds of small arms ammunition was virtually given to the enemy. This did not augur well for O'okiep as Shelton realized that Smuts' strategy would be to throw dynamite bombs onto the blockhouse roofs. The first of the chain of blockhouses, which encircled the mining town, was attacked on 9 April 1902. Eleven days into the siege, O'okiep was still holding out but casualties were mounting, and a relief force set out from Port Nolloth. By 25 April, General Smuts advised that he was about to leave the area and take part in peace negotiations in Vereeniging but that General S G Maritz was to take over the command of the besieging forces. This was not good news for O'okiep because it meant the siege would continue and the town would be attacked. Manie Maritz was determined to take the town and the valuable

Colonel Shelton's camp at O'okiep

Colonel W S Shelton was appointed by Sir Alfred Milner, British High Commissioner, in January 1901 to organize the defence of Namaqualand. His garrison was stationed at O'okiep and he developed a system of blockhouses on the outskirts of strategic towns and along the railway line to Port Nolloth. He successfully repelled the Boer invasion by defending O'okiep through the month-long siege which ended in May 1902, just before the Peace of Vereeniging was signed.
Tudor collection, Manuscripts & Archives, UCT

copper mines. He attempted by means of a decoy to blow up the O'okiep garrison, but failed. O'okiep held out and the Boers finally withdrew. On 4 May, after 30 days, the siege of O'okiep was raised, and on 31 May 1902 peace was signed at Vereeniging.[10] The damage to the mines was assessed. The mines at O'okiep were not damaged but those at Nababeep were. The railway line to Port Nolloth was badly damaged and the Cape Copper Company suffered great losses in production during the siege.

According to Deneys Reitz, who served under Smuts during the war, Manie Maritz was 'a policeman from Johannesburg, who, after many adventures, had established himself in Namaqualand as a leader of various rebel bands. He was a short, dark man, of enormous physical strength, cruel and ruthless in his methods, but a splendid guerrilla leader, and according to his lights, an ardent patriot'.[11] He would continue to feature at various times in Namaqualand's history.

The local people suffered greatly during this period. As well as the embargo on trade to prevent the Boers from hijacking supplies, there was a drought in the region and a resultant failure of crops. There was no grain or seed for planting. The mission towns of Spectakel and Komaggas were particularly badly hit because, being situated on one of the flanks of the Boer movement, they were pressured by both sides. In March 1902, for instance, it was reported that stock, grain, cows, calves, horses and hay, wagons and carts were taken by the British and in June of that year a shopkeeper in Komaggas reported he was cleaned out of his last three bags of wheat by the Boers.[12] However, 'the most searing conflation of property destruction and personal assault occurred at the Methodist mission station of Leliefontein'[13] in January 1902. An attempt by Manie Maritz and a small group of his commando to secure the submissive allegiance of the mission inhabitants to the Republican cause deteriorated into an armed confrontation, resulting in several deaths on both sides. Two days later Maritz returned with an enlarged force and attacked the mission station with extreme savagery and violence, destroying and burning everything in sight. The mission was completely destroyed and its surviving inhabitants forced to flee.

Guardsmen in the Anglo-Boer War

Town Guards were formed by the British during the Anglo-Boer War and Joseph Dembitzer served as town guard for O'okiep. He is featured somewhere in this photo.
Max Dembitzer collection

After the war, the Cape Colony was in bad shape. Many men lost their jobs in the cities and looked again to the country regions for opportunities to improve their circumstances. People were drawn to Namaqualand from all over the country.

According to the records, there were 34 Jewish men working in Namaqualand at that time. Despite the war, the search for minerals had continued. Prospecting licenses before the war indicate there was a belief that gold was to be found in the Richtersveld. Jewish names such as J Jacobson, S Greenbaum, D Stern, J Dembitzer, J G Fisher and K Kramer appear in the Register of Prospectors in 1892.[14] Whole families signed up, including wives, to extend their options. Hotels were developed from Garies to Port Nolloth and stores were built.[15] In contrast with the rest of the Colony, the villages took on a new lease of life. The Jews were to play an increasingly important rôle in their growth.

M Caplan, General Merchant, Steinkopf

Mick Caplan, the youngest of the brothers, was 'stable, focused, clever and good with his hands'. He built up quite a thriving business at this mission station, where he stayed with his wife, Yetta, for many years.
Maureen Miller collection

6 SHOPKEEPERS AND HOTELIERS

After the War, the traders in Namaqualand resumed business. The early part of the twentieth century would see an influx of personalities who spread out into the service industries.

Paul Kahn was discharged from the British army and took up smousing again. By 1907 he was able to bring his wife, Ethel Fanny and daughter, Fay, to join him in Steinkopf. It was seven years since he had left Ethel, expecting their first child, in Klein Bechstein, Latvia. Five more children were born to the couple between 1908 and 1916 and in that time they moved to Grootmis, on the Buffels River close to the coast, where he ran a shop, did some small farming and bred sheep, goats and cattle. Finally, in 1920 the family moved to Komaggas, the mission station, where they spent many years. Komaggas was described by the German missionary, J H Schmelen, when he first set eyes on it after a long trip through the dry *veld* in 1894, as an unexpectedly '*lieflike plek*' (lovely place) a veritable oasis in the desert. The church was situated at the foot of the mountain and behind it, in its protective shadow, were the houses cool under the shade of date palms and fruit trees that bore the sweetest fruit.[1]

More Jews were arriving from Eastern Europe as economic conditions, *pogroms* and mandatory army service drove them to seek greener pastures. Max Rabie arrived from Birzac, Lithuania, in 1902. His career followed a similar pattern to Paul Kahn's – he smoused in the area from 1902, opened a shop in Steinkopf in 1906 and moved to Komaggas in 1913 where he stayed until 1922. Life was hard for his wife, Margaret. She came from Paarl which was the 'centre of Jewish life' at that time, and her feelings when she encountered Steinkopf, according to her son Daniel, were 'impossible to describe'. When she asked her husband where their house was, he replied 'You're standing on the doorstep'. It was a *sink* (corrugated iron) house with *bokmis* (goat dung) on the floors – the local equivalent of Persian carpets, Daniel quipped later. Eventually the family moved to Cape Town, where Max founded the House of Fairweather, manufacturing women's clothing with the help of his five sons (and employing 700 workers at one stage). While in Namaqualand, Max often wore riding breeches – the locals, misunderstanding the patched detail on his trousers, called him '*lapgat*' Rabie. Herman, Max's brother, came out from Lithuania in 1916 and worked for him. When Max left for Cape Town, he left his business in Komaggas to Herman who stayed on for a few years.

David Gelb came to South Africa from Lithuania sometime before 1908 – his name is mentioned as one of those who formed the Zionist Society in Garies that

Komaggas

Komaggas, originally a farm belonging to Jasper Cloete, became a Coloured reserve in 1829 under the London Missionary Society followed by the Rhenish Mission from 1843. Komaggas was near the copper mine of Spectakel and it was here that Paul Kahn opened his store. The Buffels River runs through the settlement and Ethel & Paul Kahn's daughters recalled the 'divine peaches, oranges, crystal grapes, mulberries, sweet melons and water melons' that grew in the dry river bed. There was a boarding school in Komaggas that served the outlying farming district so the Kahn children did not lack companionship.
Mc Millan collection, Manuscripts & Archives, UCT

Ethel and Paul Kahn

Paul and his wife, Ethel Fanny, were separated for five years while he established himself in Namaqualand. Ethel was anxious to join him, as she was only eighteen years old when he left her pregnant with their first child in Latvia. While still smousing, he wrote pleading that he did not yet have a home for them and that he slept under the 'nearest bush' and her response was 'the bush under which you put your head, I want to put my head'. 'That's love', said their daughter, Mina, years later.
Kahn family collection

Dan Rabie in Komaggas

Six-year-old Daniel Rabie, son of Max and Margaret in a formal photograph on his tricycle by Steven McNally, itinerant photographer from Cape Town. Daniel's pet calf is not pictured in this photo! A *mohel* was sent for, from Cape Town, for the *brith milah* of each of Max Rabie's sons born in Namaqualand and they had their *barmitzvahs* in Cape Town. Seven of Max and Margaret's nine children were born in Namaqualand.
Dan Rabie collection

year.[2] He was in his early twenties and was helped on his way by the wholesale firm of Brown Lawrence in Cape Town. His uncle, Abraham Gelb of Stellenbosch, thought he had more chance of making a living in Namaqualand, where there was a mine, than in the Cape, which was 'in the doldrums'. With the few pounds he had, David bought a horse and cart and with the help of a Coloured assistant, went smousing from farm to farm. 'It took a lot of guts' said his son Raphael later, after all 'he couldn't speak English or Afrikaans'. After a short stint at smousing, like many Jews before him, he was able to buy a shop with a house attached from a German pioneering couple in Concordia, a copper-mining town.

Just before the First World War broke out David went back to Lithuania to arrange to bring his brothers out to South Africa. On his return via England, he stayed in Manchester with a cousin and there he met Millie Sippert whom he persuaded (it took him three or four months) to join him in South Africa. In those days the train from Cape Town went only as far as Eendekuil (near Citrusdal) and from there travel was by horse and cart. Millie later said that it took almost as long to get from Eendekuil to Concordia as it had from Manchester to Cape Town. It was 'endless' and she cried all the way. Millie became one of a unique generation of wives whose strength and connection with Namaqualand was formidable. As her son, Raphael, later said, 'she withstood it'.

The Caplan brothers, Harry, Caple and Mick, came from Newport, Wales. Harry was the first, coming out sometime before 1906, followed by the others. Caple had been an apprentice baker in Wales, sleeping under the counter in the bakery – much like the store clerks in the next decade in Namaqualand. Mick, who 'knew how to handle himself'[3] learned his skills in the boxing trade, taking on boxers at English funfairs and knocking them out for sixpence pocket money. After a stint in O'okiep, Mick opened a store in Steinkopf. His store became quite a thriving business. He was clever and very good

Florrie Caplan

Florrie Caplan, wife of Caple, with her infant son Victor, who was born in O'okiep in 1914. She was described by Victor's wife as a dignified and cultured woman who loved music.
Caplan family collection

Three chaps fooling around

Immigrants from Wales, these three Caplan brothers, Caple on the left, Harry on the right and Mick between them, are pictured in O'okiep in the first decade of the twentieth century. They were a lively bunch. Harry died young, Mick opened a store in Steinkopf and Caple spent many years there trying his hand at shopkeeping, prospecting and hotel keeping.
Maureen Miller collection

Concordia circa 1880

Concordia was a mining town that grew up around two copper mines, the Hester Maria and the Wheel Julia. Albert van Schlicht, the German mineralogist, originally built the village to accomodate miners from Cornwall. The village became a thriving community where a 'Cornish way of life was pursued with some vigour' – sport, recreational activities such as picnics and horse racing and Cornish cuisine such as the Cornish pasty became a way of life in Namaqualand. (Dickason, *Cornish immigrants*, p.33.)
Gogh album

Farming families in the Kamiesberge

Farming families such as these living isolated lives in the Kamiesberg would come down, infrequently, to the village to buy goods. A ritual followed the arrival of the farmer and his wife at the local store. Tea was served by the storekeeper's wife, some exchange of news took place relating to the weather, the state of health of the family and financial matters. Only then would the business of trade begin. The farmer would bring with him farm products for trading such as butter, eggs, poultry, skins (dassie, jackal, baboon and goat) and would barter or trade them for goods from the shop.
Kotze, P N, Doctoral Thesis. University of Stellenbosch. 1942

Truck loading skins

Skins being loaded on to a truck in Concordia. Skins were an important trading item for shopkeepers. Years later Pauline Saharin recalled the interior of her father's shop in Nababeep – the drying skins brought in by farmers to sell, 'the wonderful smells of raw tobacco and the food, bales of clothes and sacks of mielies and corn piled up … and the sound of the old silver cash register.'
Morris Boiskin collection

Masonic Hotel, Springbok

There were many Masonic Hotels in the country areas started or owned by masons, who named or renamed them Masonic Hotel to attract visiting masons. Many commercial travellers were masons and sought out these hotels to connect with fellow masons or obtain information on Lodge activities in the town. Country hotels became the centre of village life. They were 'home from home' for travellers and boarders; they became the centre for Jewish celebrations for widely dispersed congregations, such as the one in Namaqualand, with people coming from neighbouring towns to take part in the High Festivals, weddings, *barmitzvahs* and reunion dinners (later); and they provided entertainment for the locals (regular card games such as rummy). Very often, the hoteliers and their families lived in the hotels and participated generously in the life of the hotel.
Cissie Rakoff collection

Phoenix Lodge 1910

Phoenix Lodge Brothers in 1910 with three Jewish members, Harry Schur (son of Moses Schur), Jacob Frank (a lawyer) and Harry Caplan. Masonry was started in Namaqualand in 1864 by a Cornishman, W W Townsend. Among foundation members were significant names in Namaqualand history such as Albert van Schlicht, Richard Carstens and Charles A Pilkington. In the next century many Jewish names would appear in the records of the Lodge, many serving as Master. Note 21of the 26 members are sporting handlebar moustaches, highly fashionable at that time.
Phoenix Lodge Celebration Souvenir, 1885-1985

with his hands and was responsible for the electrification of Steinkopf and also laid the water pipes. He married a Londoner, Yetta Paepert. Caple married her sister, Florrie, and joined Mick in the Steinkopf store for a while.

In 1904 census figures record that there were 40 Jews (38 men and 2 women) resident in Namaqualand out of a total population of 20 041 (of which 5 004 were white). The population growth, particularly as far as the Jews were concerned, was steady and by 1918 the number of Jews had risen to 135 (86 men and 49 women).[4]

The primary economic activity of these shopkeepers was trading, mainly in skins, but the farmers also brought other goods for bartering – wheat, wool, butter, eggs, hand-made leather cushions and *karosses*. Very often both the farmer and his wife would be wearing trousers made of tanned goatskin when they came to the *dorp* to do business. In addition to the trading function, the early shopkeepers also acted as informal 'bankers' to the farmers, (a function universally played out by Jewish shopkeepers in the country) helping them during difficult times by extending credit or attaching their farms until they were in a position to repossess them – the farmers continued to live on the farm but it was owned by the shopkeeper and no money passed hands. Many Namaqualand farmers tell this story, saying that under such circumstances they would have had a '*saai plaas maar nie 'n oes plaas nie*'.[5]

The nineteenth century had not been an easy time for Namaqualand farmers. In addition to the endemic problems of lack of water and grazing land, they were plagued by locusts and the massive springbok migrations (*trekbokken*), which decimated the land. Modern methods of controlling these pests, which evolved in the twentieth century, did not exist then. So the assistance of the Jewish 'financiers' was very welcome.

Apart from the shopkeepers, a new breed of Jewish entrepreneur was appearing, namely the hotelier. The hospitality business was not as unfamiliar an occupation as one would imagine – running an inn or tavern was an occupation already familiar to Jews in the Pale of Settlement of Eastern Europe. During the mid-nineteenth century some Jewish businessmen were given licenses by Russian noblemen to run canteens or taverns in the rural areas. In the urban areas of Russia, some Jewish traders were well known as sellers of alcohol to factory workers. In South Africa, liquor trading and hotels were strongly connected. Although in the country, hotels or inns essentially provided boarding facilities to serve the traders, commercial travellers and civil servants of developing communities, selling liquor was an important aspect of making a profit.[6]

By the end of their first decade in Namaqualand, Jews ran the hotels from Bitterfontein to Port Nolloth. It was called 'having a wine and spirit license with privileges'.[7] These establishments offered clean and comfortable conditions and hospitality. The Garies Hotel, run by the Rosenbergs, had six bedrooms, two stables for 18 horses, a billiard room and a bar (also a canteen 'for the natives'). M Schur & Son's hotel in Bowesdorp, run by Joseph Schur, consisted of nine bedrooms, two sitting rooms, a dining room, two kitchens, stabling for 36 horses, a bar and a private bar.

In the early years of Springbokfontein, (the name of the town was officially changed to Springbok in 1911) the lone establishment was owned by Alfred James Loynes. It was really a boarding house where civil servants attached to the magistrate's court, and some teachers stayed. During the Anglo-Boer War, it served as a rounding-up place for prisoners of war. Loynes' establishment became the Masonic Hotel and by 1915 was owned by Bernard Slesing and Sam Grodzinsky, business partners who also had a store. The hotel was situated in the clearing where there had once been a natural spring, one of the watering holes of the immense herds of springbok found in Namaqualand in the early days – hence the name of the town Springbokfontein – but, by now, wiped out by years of hunting. Slesing and Grodzinsky moved into their new hotel in Springbok and ran it for some time. Slesing brought his nephew,

Birmingham Villa, Kamieskroon

On the steps of the Birmingham Villa hotel in Kamieskroon circa 1927. The hotel derived its name from the hometown of Solomon Josephson, one of the two partners who ran the hotel.
Top L-R: Mark Tombuk, Minnie Schapera, Esther Josephson, Annie Abramson (Max Schapera's sister) and Max Schapera (the other partner in the hotel).
Bottom L-R: Children Raphael, Roy and Marion Schapera.
Raphael Schapera collection

Max Shapiro, down from then-Rhodesia and set him up in the hotel. Under 'Shappy', the hotel would become famous in the annals of country hotels. There is a story that, in 1915, during the days of the rebellion in South West Africa, Manie Maritz is reputed to have set himself up on the *koppie* (small hill) in the square and 'sniped through a window at the bottles in Shappy's bar nearby until liquor ran into the sandy street'.[8] The hotel came to be regarded as an oasis in the desert and was renowned for its excellent food, service and upkeep. Shappy was a gifted hotelier and a natural host. He had a wonderful sense of humour and loved a good bit of fun or a practical joke. He treated guests with spectacular old-fashioned hospitality. He eventually bought the establishment in 1931.

The commercial travellers, heirs of the *smouse*, made very good use of the hotels which would become their home away from home. Having to cope with long

Commercial travellers 1920

Commercial travellers staying at the hotel in Bowesdorp 1920. Their country hosts were S Josephson and M Schapera, proprietors of the hotel (1st and 2nd right). Notice the Eaton Robins truck – wholesale merchants in Cape Town who supplied the *smouse* and commercial travellers. By 1930, the firm had gone out of business. Other wholesale merchants like Jagger & Co and M Bloch and Co, also supplied the storekeepers.
Raphael Schapera collection

itineraries and bad roads, they could only 'work' one or two *dorps* a day and were often away from their families for long periods. Some had specially constructed cars, which carried rails of men's suits, or goods could be transported in 'whisker skips'. They visited the little *dorps* and stayed at the local hotels. Some of the *platteland* hotels had special 'sample' rooms, which the commercial travellers could hire to display their wares. Travellers often formed rotating poker schools, playing each night, and sometimes through the night, at a different hotel, where the hotelier – much to the disgust of his wife – often joined in enthusiastically. Rummy schools were also popular. The Namaqualand Hebrew Congregation benefited regularly from donations made by '5 hands' – as revealed by entries in the *schenodering* (donations) book in the early 1920s.

The hotels became the centre of the social life of the community, and the hoteliers found themselves in key positions as the orchestrators of community living. In fact, the hoteliers wielded a unique power since they always knew the business of everyone in the *dorp* and became the channels through which gossip, information and community news would flow. Indeed, as businesspeople and social convenors, the hoteliers greatly enhanced the life of the Namaqualand communities.[10]

The Jewish hoteliers and shopkeepers played an important role in the area – bringing to it a service that was new and much required. These new services were appreciated and extensively used by the whole community. They also greatly assisted the integration of the Jews into the community ensuring the development of respect and friendship between Jews and Gentiles. It was the beginning of a legacy of Jewish hoteliers in South Africa that would span a hundred years.

Max Shapiro and friends

Max Shapiro, centre front, with friends. 'Shappy' as Max Shapiro was popularly known, ran the Masonic Hotel in Springbok from 1913 until his death in 1963. He was a gifted hotelier and natural host. He also was one of the worst pranksters in the district. In one incident, he is reputed to have stolen the *Rosh Hashanah* meal from the kitchen of Boris Saharin while the *shul* service was being conducted and 'saved the day' for the kindly but unsuspecting Boris by inviting him and his guests for lunch at his hotel where he served a grand meal.
Selina Gordon collection

Bowesdorp village

Bowesdorp, site of the mother church of the Dutch Reformed Church in Namaqualand, was situated in a small narrow valley, completely surrounded by hills. Bleak and arid, the region was bitterly cold in winter and very hot in summer. In the early days, the little village had a church, school with hostel, tiny post office, police station, small hotel, two general stores, eight houses and six or seven reed huts. The photo shows the hotel, store and adjoining buildings of M Schur & Son and a tennis court in front. After the water supply dried up in the late 1800s, a decision was taken to move the entire village to Kamieskroon (six kilometres away) and to rebuild the church and school. This was achieved by 1924.
Raphael Schapera collection

Wedding of Joseph and Rebecca Galombik

Rebecca Palley was only eighteen years old when she came from Russia to her brother in Cape Town. He died shortly afterwards. She married Joseph Galombik in her early twenties and this, their wedding photograph, shows her to be a beautiful and stylish woman. Joseph died in 1925 and Rebecca was left with four small children, Solly aged eight years, Belle, aged five years, Arnold, aged four years and Ita, only two years old.
Belle Flax collection

7 LIFE IN THE BUNDU

The early Jews who established themselves in Namaqualand as traders, shopkeepers and hoteliers often arrived in the area alone, sole travellers intent on finding a new life. Once settled, they would find wives overseas or at the Cape, and bring them back to Namaqualand. It was not easy for these women. It was 'life in the *bundu*' (wild open country) according to one local.[1]

Marian van Niekerk, the wife of the district surgeon, describes life in Namaqualand in those early days:[2]

> To those who entered Namaqualand for the first time in the early twenties, the arid barrenness, loneliness and utter 'beyondness' of the country ... was a disillusionment for them. Facilities were minimal; lighting by candles and lamps; always a scarcity of water – obtained from two fountains and two public bore holes and brought to the various homes in tubs on wheels @ 1 shilling per 60 gallons; shower buckets for bathing purposes and the tub system of sewerage removal; cooking on paraffin, wood or coal stoves; food kept cool in a 'kokerboom' (quiver tree) or a coal system with continuous water running over coal; fresh vegetables were scarce, bread self-baked... Medical facilities were primitive. The district area was large and doctors scarce – one district surgeon and one mine doctor. Women in childbirth suffered a lot. Birth deliverances were often undertaken by the 'old woman' – with the lack of better services they did good work but many lives were lost through white leg and other birth sufferings. Tuberculosis was rife and many succumbed to the disease. Telephones and communications were few and far between, this made medical services a nightmare at times. . . . The kokerboom would be hollowed out, and lined with a framework of mesh, then coal would be placed at the bottom, topped with sacking which would be continually kept wet and through evaporation would keep the contents cool. It had the advantage of being portable.

Galombik children

The four Galombik children on the farm outside Kamieskroon, where all four were born. Belle recalled the farmhouse with a big stoep and lots of plants, its three 'huge' rooms and a 'huge' kitchen (a child's view!) The kitchen had a coal stove and a clay floor where they washed in a large zinc bath. *Yvonne Galombik collection*

The women worked very hard. They assisted their husbands in the shops and hotels. Travellers would arrive at any time of the day or night and the hoteliers' wives would feed them, even if it was at one o'clock in the morning. These women were real *baleboste* (capable women) and were often responsible for the success of the hotel. In most of the country hotels the catering was outstanding, even famous. The finest Jewish cooking was often provided – dinner menus could consist of two soups, pickled herrings, steamed fish, curried fish, Irish

Jenny Schur, pictured with her husband, Joseph

Despite living conditions in Namaqualand in the early years women, such as Florrie Caplan and Jenny Schur, still managed to look beautiful and elegant. This photo of Jenny Schur, probably wearing her wedding dress, shows her to be a stylish city girl. *Clara Schur collection*

stew – cooked the Jewish way, braised lamb cutlets, sauté of giblets, fried chops, roast leg of mutton and guava jelly, roast turkey, roast lamb and apricot sauce, half a dozen different vegetables, puddings, sweets and coffee.[3] The hoteliers and their families offered old-fashioned hospitality and so the hotels became home away from home for those who boarded there permanently or passed through regularly. Life for the children of these hoteliers was not easy. Their parents were always working and they had no family life to speak of. The two daughters of one such hard-working hotelier couple remembered envying a family who lived an isolated life on a farm in the Kamiesberg because of their close family life, and they savoured the special occasions they spent with them there.

Some wives even managed the stores on their own when the need arose. Rebecca Galombik, for instance, continued running the farm and shop at Rietkloof outside Kamieskroon after her husband, Joseph, died suddenly in 1928 leaving her with four young children to support. She grew wheat and maize and also ran a shop that sold farm products and other general goods needed by the farm labourers. Her children attended school in Kamieskroon and boarded with a local family during the week. They travelled by horse and cart on Mondays to Kamieskroon and back home to the farm on Fridays. Her elder son, Solly, was eight years old when his father died. He adopted the mantle of man of the house, and helped his mother in the shop, kept the farm books, and, according to his sister, Belle Flax, 'did everything'. Solly only spoke Afrikaans so when it was time for him to study for his *barmitzvah*, (religious ceremony on reaching thirteen) his mother sent him to Cape Town for a year where he attended Jan van Riebeeck, the Afrikaans-medium school. Thereafter, he rejoined his family in Vanrhynsdorp, where they were now living in order to be part of a larger Jewish community, and celebrated his *barmitzvah* there. He and Belle both matriculated in Vanrhynsdorp and the family then moved to Cape Town where Arnold, their younger sibling, finished his schooling at the South African College School (SACS). The farms in Namaqualand were leased out to provide an income for the family. Arnold excelled at sport and was made a prefect after only one year at SACS. The boys went on to become brilliant lawyers in Cape Town. In their subsequent careers they earned the trust and confidence of many Namaqualanders.

Rebecca Galombik must have been a woman of resourcefulness and fortitude and obviously had a good business brain. There are many other examples of women of similar calibre in Namaqualand at that time. Jenny Schur, wife of Joseph, managed the store in Nababeep while her husband was buying up skins for the Cape Town wholesaler, J W Jagger & Co, in Bushmanland and around Namaqualand in the 1920s.

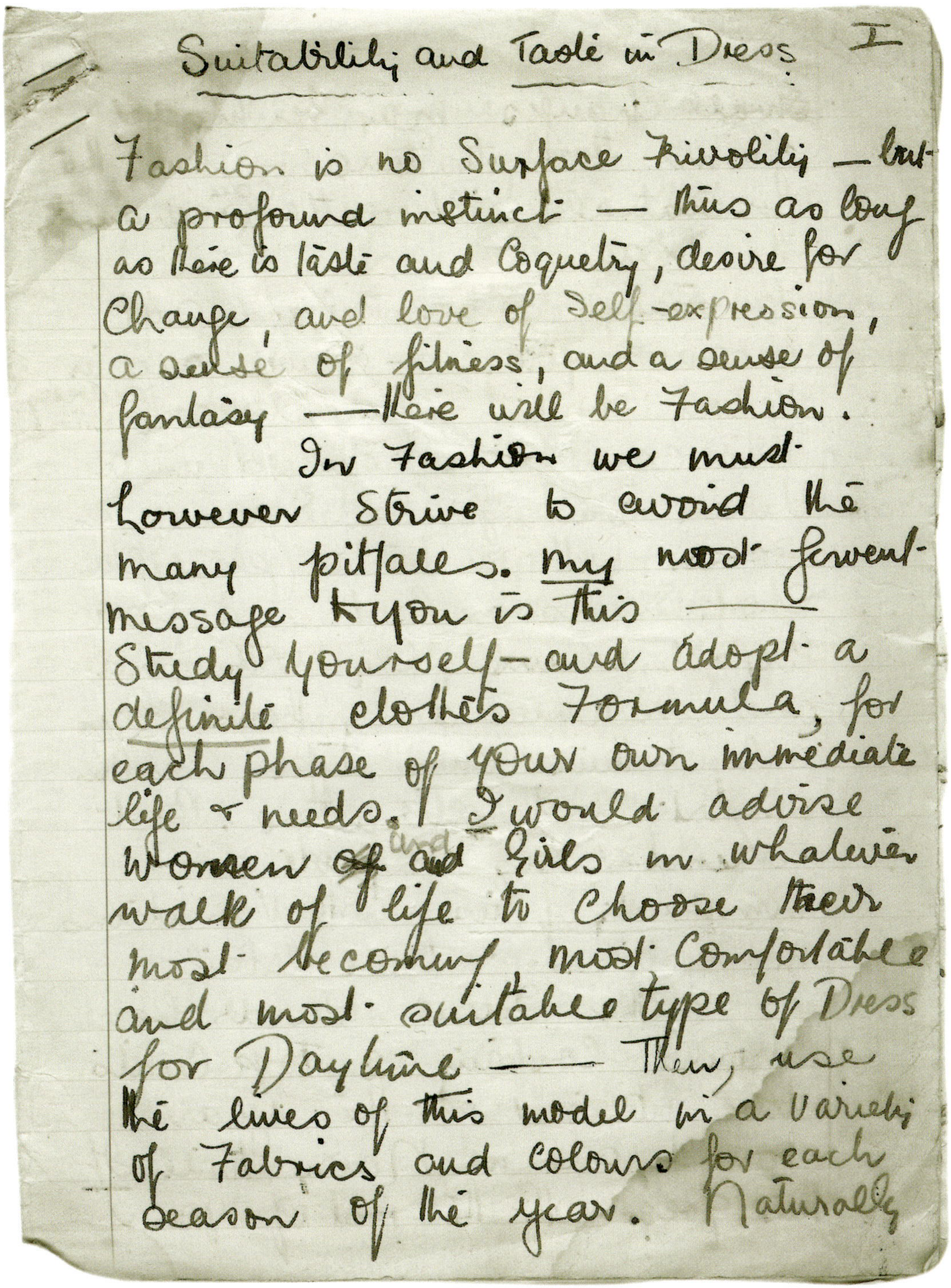

Suitability and Taste in Dress I

Fashion is no Surface Frivolity — but a profound instinct — thus as long as there is taste and Coquetry, desire for Change, and love of Self-expression, a sense of fitness, and a sense of fantasy — there will be Fashion.

In Fashion we must however Strive to avoid the many pitfalls. My most fervent message to you is this — Study yourself — and adopt a definite clothes Formula, for each phase of your own immediate life & needs. I would advise Women ~~of~~ and Girls in whatever walk of life to choose their most becoming most Comfortable and most suitable type of Dress for Daytime — Then, use the lines of this model in a Variety of Fabrics and colours for each season of the year. Naturally

Extract from Rae Rosenberg's scrapbook

An extract from the etiquette and fashion scrapbook compiled by Rae Rosenberg of Garies for her talks to the local Women's Agricultural Union, the VLV, in the 1930s.
Marlene Sacks collection

Exterior of Solomon Rabinowitz's store

Exterior of Solomon Rabinowitz's store at Steinkopf with Pegasus petrol pumps in front. Dinah, Solomon's wife, often managed the store on her own when her husband was away in the Richtersveld prospecting for minerals. 'My dear wife sacrificed her youth in Namaqualand with me' he wrote later.
Benjamin Rabinowitz collection

The Rosenberg's home in Garies

'Everyone had *Yomtov* together in the forties in Max and Rae Rosenberg's home in Garies – the Abrahamsons, the Pachters and Sammy Shirk, the store clerk' said their daughter Marlene Sacks.
Rosenberg family collection

Max Rosenberg's shop

Max Rosenberg, who took over the hotel and shop from his parents, Philip and Minnie, spent long hours in the shop and Sundays were for the bookkeeping. Arthur Rosenberg remembered the barrels of Dutch herring packed in salt in wooden containers from Holland. His mother, Rae, made chopped herring and, even in the 1990s, Arthur vividly recalled the flavour.
Rosenberg family collection

Dinah Rabinowitz, wife of Solomon Rabinowitz, a mineral prospector who would feature in the diamond story (see chapter 9) and whom she married in 1913, ran the store in Steinkopf for many years while her husband prospected for minerals in the Richtersveld. According to her daughter, Isabel, she lived a solitary life, with only her regular family correspondence and the week-old newspapers to sustain her and keep her in touch with civilization. Carel Birkby wrote of her: 'Rabinowitz's wife provided a superb meal for so desolate a spot. Sixty miles from the sea, she had fish baked as a city chef might do it; the best mutton in the country; canned peaches and cream – but not from a Namaqualand cow'.[4] 'Later', he continued, 'she sat down to a fine piano and played tunes from Edwardian musical comedies, tunes she learned – twenty years ago – before she came to Namaqualand to share her husband's pioneering life'. Similarly, Ellen Rabinowitz, wife of Louis, also ran the store in Port Nolloth while her husband attended to his farm near Kniebrandt, a short distance from the bottom of the Anenous Pass.

It must have been particularly hard for those women from the cities for whom Namaqualand represented a startling contrast to the sophistication and convenience of urban living. Rae Rosenberg, wife of Max Rosenberg of the Garies Hotel, was a cultured woman trained in music and painting in Cape Town. She had a great sense of style and became well known for being an excellent advisor on *aanneming* (confirmation) clothes for church – ordering and supplying the appropriate shoes, hats and clothes from the shop adjoining the hotel that she ran. She shared her city experience and flair for food, clothes and etiquette with the local women by joining the Vroue Landbou Vereniging (Women's Agricultural Association) and creating a scrapbook of recipes, fashion styles and etiquette.

Rae Rosenberg was a colourful character. She would try imaginative ways of getting her message across at special meetings in the town. So, for example, she made up a soldier's costume, and wore it at a meeting to pro-

Millie Gelb with her children

Millie Gelb, wife of David Gelb, and their four children, L-R Ivan, Harold (standing), Natalie, Millie and Raphael, circa 1929. The family lived in Concordia where all four children were born at home with the local doctor in attendance. Raphael Gelb remembered all four having their tonsils out on the same day – on the kitchen table. The doctor from Vanrhynsdorp travelled to Concordia to assist Dr Cowan. In 1933 the family moved to Springbok.
Raphael & Thelma Gelb collection

mote the SAWAS work during the Second World War, and she made and wore a Voortrekker costume for the centenary celebration of the Great Trek, according to her daughter, Marlene Sacks. She regularly invited the local Coloured school principal for tea so he could practice his English – Frikkie Smit said it was the only place he could speak English. Many years later, Mr Smit would visit Rae in the Jewish Aged Home in Cape Town.

Another city girl was Millie Gelb, from Manchester, England, who came to Concordia in 1914. She bore David four children in Concordia within the space of six years: Harold in 1915, Ivan in 1916, Raphael in 1918 and finally their sister Natalie (whom they called Baba) in 1920, all born at home with the local doctor in attendance. Millie assisted her husband in the shop after the Depression despite never learning to speak Afrikaans – luckily they had a Coloured assistant called Piet Macada who understood her perfectly. The family said later they could never imagine how he knew what she wanted. She also had atrocious handwriting and only Piet could interpret her entries in the invoice book! It was a 'helluva life', said her son, Raphael, later. The children started school in Concordia – five classes in one room, up to standard six, with only one teacher. Their friends were the Coloured children – there were no colour barriers then. Raphael remembers climbing the mountains and *koppies* around the town, picnicking, camping and outings with the Boy Scouts, playing soccer and cricket.

Recipe from a tannie-doktor for treating sepsis of the foot:

Mix sunlight soap, bread crumbs, mealie pap and sugar (optional)

Make a paste and place over the area infected by the thorn.

Leave overnight.

Three years after the Concordia mine closed down, in 1933, the Gelbs moved to Springbok and established themselves there.

For the children growing up, it was a 'charmed childhood'. Raphael Schapera remembers his childhood in Bowesdorp in the little valley: playing in the river and the trees – and also the police station which was the coolest part of the village; seeing the camels of the police patrol; and hearing stories of hunting from the men who came to talk and shop at his father's store. He remembers 'a cameo of lots of heroes', and the 'mystery of playing with the coloured children learning all about the roots and the berries and the plants in the mountains and living with baboons coming down, living with snakes in the valley' – learning about the culture and traditions of the earliest inhabitants of that area and developing a respect for the environment.[5]

As far as health care was concerned, when doctors were not available, or could not be reached, the local *tannie-doktors* would be called upon to assist. They had standard prescriptions for pneumonia, tuberculosis and sepsis. Raphael Schapera remembers, as a very young child in Bowesdorp, being wrapped in warm skin of a freshly slaughtered sheep – the local *tannie-doktor's* standard prescription for pneumonia! Other remedies prescribed by Mrs Visser, who was the policeman's wife, were bread poultices and sugar poultices for septic foot sores. Raphael said 'I was a child of two and here was my mother, a young woman, having a child that was ill and these were the kinds of conditions under which she was raising a family'. Rebecca Galombik's youngest child, Ita, died of a burst appendix, mis-diagnosed as having eaten too much green fruit. She was only nine years old. Victims of tuberculosis among the Jews included Raphael Schapera's cousin, Herman, and his grandmother, Rachel. It was not only primitive treatment but

Women on the rocks

Time out for hard-working pioneering wives. L-R: Millie Gelb, Dinah Rabinowitz, Leah Klass, Leah Albert, Ellen Rabinowitz and Gertie Rabinowitz.
Hyme Rabinowitz collection

also lack of information about symptoms that caused so many fatalities.

Despite the difficulties of living there, many of the women loved Namaqualand. They were the 'happiest days of our lives' for some, such as Polly, wife of lawyer Jacob Frank. These were inevitably the women who made the best of it – Minnie Schapera, Max Schapera's wife, for instance and Dinah Rabinowitz who loved music and later said that life in Steinkopf wasn't so bad – 'after all, we had a piano'.

The Jewish woman was important as partner, helpmate, mother and significant member of a social network both within and outside the Jewish circle in Namaqualand. Her involvement was crucial to her husband's success. Even the business of buying and selling, typically the husband's prerogative, involved the wives – *geselskap* (conversation) over cups of tea mainly concerning farming activity and the welfare of various members of the family (some traditional *schmoozing*), was the customary ritual preceding the serious business of buying and selling.

In the early years of Judaism in Namaqualand, when strict observance of traditional religion was not always possible, the Jewish woman's role in preserving Jewish identity and teaching Jewish values was crucial. Observance goes right back to the first *Yom Kippur* in Namaqualand celebrated in the 1850s by Esther and Aaron de Pass in the lonely port of Port Nolloth with no Jews around for miles – Esther, according to her husband, was 'strict in such matters'! Out on a limb, in Komaggas, 48 kilometres from Springbok, Margaret Rabie made *homentashen* (special cakes) for *Purim* 'if she had the *mon*' (poppy seed) and prepared for *Pesach*, receiving the *matzoth* from Cape Town. Dan Rabie, recalling his years in Namaqualand, said his father would conduct a 'proper *seder*'. The only other whites living in Komaggas at that time, apart from the Rabie family, were a missionary, a schoolteacher and the Kahn family.[6]

Dinah Rabinowitz's daughter, Isabel, wrote years later:

Scenes from Jewish family life

Rosh Hashanah in Port Nolloth at the home of Mr & Mrs Bolon, 1932. Amongst them are Mrs Leah Klass, Herman Klass, Sam Bolon, Cissie Rakoff, Linkel Rabinowitz and Sam Stein. *Cissie Rakoff collection*

> It is strange to imagine the life of a Jewish family in a Rhenish Coloured Mission Station … Dinah's father helped her to maintain her close bonds with Jewish religious life. Every week a hand-soldered tin of *kosher* meat would reach her from Cape Town. Every Friday night the candles were lit, and the children were made aware, early in life, that this meant the inauguration of the Sabbath, which had to be respected. When the acquisition of a car in later years made it possible, the Holy Days were spent in Springbok, 35 miles (56 km) away, where a flourishing Jewish community arose. It is indeed true to say that they carried Jewish civilization with them into this outpost in the desert. The *bris* (circumcision) of their eldest son was performed at Steinkopf in traditional style. A *mohel* was sent out from Cape Town by taxi – no mean feat in 1923 – and their family sent them a load of Jewish delicacies and wine to celebrate the event.[7]

Reminiscences of other Jewish women in the little

Two mothers-in-law in Garies

Two grandmothers in Garies, Luba Levy (Rae Rosenberg's mother) and Minnie Rosenberg (Max's mother) with her sons, Max and Joe.
Rosenberg family collection

country towns of the Cape, also reveal that some families were strictly *kosher*; all celebrated the Sabbath with a special meal (usually fish) on Friday nights with *kiddush* wine, white tablecloth and candles. Some women baked their own *challah* (plaited bread) and the daughters always seemed to help their mothers in the preparation of the food.[8] Some shopkeepers closed their shops on Saturdays but many did not. On the mines, for instance, the workers were paid on Saturdays so it was 'the busiest day' according to Solomon Kluk referring to his first job in Concordia.

Abe Schapera and Arthur Rosenberg both refer to the important role their mothers played. In Arthur's case, it was his grandmother too. Luba Levy, Arthur's maternal grandmother, came to live with them in Garies after her husband died and she was left all alone in Cape Town. She was committed to Judaism and she would light candles on Friday evenings and was in charge of changing the cutlery and crockery for Passover.[9] Arthur's sister, Marlene, told how she was with them 'as long as I can remember' and was 'as sweet as honey.' Arthur believes it was the grandmothers who were really the backbone of maintaining the Jewish religion in the country. Many of the Garies Jews at the time celebrated *Yomtov* (the Festival) in the Rosenberg home. Marlene recalls how 'after the main course, everyone would get up, take a stretch walking up and down the main road in Garies before returning for the traditional dessert – a nut-encrusted trifle'. The story hasn't changed much, it would seem!

Abe Schapera remembered his mother, Rachel Rose, 'in the kitchen practically all day supervising the cooking' especially when she was preparing for the High Festivals. She certainly had her work cut out since his father, Herman, was well versed in the Talmud, and had brought the first Sefer Torah to Namaqualand and their home in Garies became the informal centre for the practice of Judaism in Namaqualand. The High Festivals were regularly observed and the scene outside their home at these times according to Abe, who was born in Garies in 1906, resembled a '*Yiddishe Nagmaal* with Cape carts outspanned all over the place especially under the pepper trees'. All the guests were provided with 'delicious meals' – chicken, mutton, eggs and wholesome '*boerbrood*' – 'that home-made brown bread and a cup of coffee was a meal in itself' recalled Abe Schapera.[10] For many years until they left Namaqualand in 1911, the Schapera home in Garies was the place where Jews gathered.

It is clear that the contribution of the Jewish woman was crucial to the preservation of Judaism in Namaqualand. It was the Jewish family that provided a vehicle for Jewish identity while the informal structures of Jewish communal life were developing and before the community had grown to a size that would warrant more formal structures being put in place.

A view of Garies in the late1920s

Rosenberg family collection

Springbok in the 1920s

Springbok in the 1920s showing the town hall (on the right) where Sidney Windisch had the first bio-scope. A personal recollection of what it was like was provided by one ex-resident who remembered the children sitting on the floor in the front and the adults coping with the flimsy seating at the back. The sequence of the film reels was often mixed up making for obscure viewing. On the whole, everyone had a great time! *Betty Wright collection*

8 MILESTONES AND DUST STORMS

South Africa, being a dominion of Britain, was automatically drawn into the First World War against Germany. South Africa was the only part of the Empire with a territory contiguous to a German possession, South West Africa. On 10 August 1914 the South African Cabinet made a decision to invade German South West Africa. Opposition to this decision culminated in a rebellion among some Afrikaners under former Boer Generals. In October, S G ('Manie') Maritz, now a Lieutenant-Colonel in the Union Defence Force in charge of the north-western Cape district adjacent to South West Africa, crossed the frontier with more than a thousand Citizen Force soldiers to join the enemy. Union troops had already landed at Port Nolloth on 1 September 1914 but the invasion had to be delayed while the rebellion was suppressed. Nevertheless within six months, the South African force numbering over 40 000 men had conquered the territory and the German commander surrendered in July 1915. Manie Maritz fled to Angola but returned in 1924 and served a three-year prison sentence.[1]

There was serious dislocation after the war and in Namaqualand the closing of the copper mines aggravated the situation. The demand for copper had dropped – copper was used for the casing of bullets and shells which was no longer needed; the mines were experiencing difficulties with supplies and there was a prohibition on the export of matte or impure smelted copper ore to England. So the Cape Copper Company Ltd took a decision, implemented in 1919, to suspend its Namaqualand mining operations.[2] The entire staff was retrenched. It was a hard blow for Namaqualand, particularly since the area was experiencing a severe drought.

Transport riders during the invasion of German South West Africa, 1914

The Caplan brothers, Mick and Caple, were very adventurous. One of their enterprises involved transport riding from O'okiep to German South West Africa in 1914 whilst South African troops invaded the region. Within a year the 8000-strong German garrison there was forced to surrender and the League of Nations gave South Africa a mandate to rule the territory. The Caplan brothers were paid for their efforts with gold sovereigns.
Hyme Rabinowitz collection

During periodic drought conditions, farmers in Namaqualand tended to look to the local mines for work in order to supplement their incomes. The mines were labour intensive and could accommodate many unskilled workers. Farming in Namaqualand had always been difficult and precarious – low rainfall, drought and vermin wreaked havoc. Many farmers had by this time established themselves in the region and owned land in both the winter rainfall area of Namaqualand and the summer rainfall area of Bushmanland, and could trek with their sheep between the two. But there were others, smaller farmers, who did not have access to grazing and were badly affected when severe droughts hit the region.[3] In the early years they then took to transport riding or working on the mines to tide themselves over these difficult times and would return to their farms

Alfred Levy in uniform during the First World War

Alfred Levy, brother of Phillip Levy, in Royal Flying Corps uniform during the First World War.
David Levy collection

Prisoners of war

Phillip Levy, front row left, prisoner of war in German South West Africa during the First World War. At the time he was serving under General Manie Maritz, who had been appointed to head up a strong force of mostly members of the Active Citizen Force from a training camp in Upington. Once over the border, Maritz went into rebellion against the Union Government and openly sided with the Germans. He was already in collaboration with the Germans and had, in fact, adopted German citizenship in South West Africa. His actions were attributed to resentment at the loss of his country's independence to the British and his wish to restore the old Boer republics. Many of his men refused to follow him – among them Phillip Levy – and they were interned by the Germans. Maritz and his reduced force briefly occupied Keimoes, Kakamas and Kenhardt and sent attachments to Calvinia and Upington but they were finally defeated by the Union Defence Force at Kakamas.
David Levy collection

when conditions improved.

So abject were conditions in the early twenties that it was reported that the local population could not afford to clothe themselves and the more 'modest' females were too ashamed even to come into the villages.[4]

The desolation in the district is vividly portrayed in a poem by the famous prospector, Fred Cornell:

Namaqualand 1920

A land of mountains and scorched up plain
Where there is nothing to do but pray for rain
Parched and barren and choked with sand
Lonely deserted Namaqualand
With a long white road, that winds its way
Where the dust-storms blind and the sand-whirls play
And the mirage flickers on every hand
Of the pitiless path through Namaqualand.[5]

Fred Cornell

The Divisional Council appealed to the Cape Government to consider extending the railway line from Klawer to Namaqualand in order to give work to the locals. The appeal was turned down but the Administrator of the Cape encouraged the establish-

ment of a support committee for the retrenched mine workers and offered separate funding. This was duly done and the Council was able to distribute food and clothing, procure seed and organize road maintenance projects and so help alleviate the suffering of the local population.

During the war years, more and more Jews had left the Cape and found their way to Namaqualand hoping to find work. This trend was accelerated with demobilization when the war ended, so that by 1918, the number of Jews in Namaqualand had reached 135.[6] There was a developing Jewish infrastructure which attracted them. Already in 1908, a Zionist Society had been formed in Garies. Its members were Herman Schapera, David Gelb, Joseph Galombik, Philip Rosenberg, A Chodos, M Kaplan, W Assen, J Ginsberg and E Bernstine. It is interesting to note that two non-Jews also joined: J Denyssen, the one-time Resident Magistrate of Namaqualand and J de Bruyn.[7] The Zionist movement, to secure the Jewish return to the land of Israel,[8] had begun in 1898 but it was the first Zionist Conference in South Africa, held in 1905,[9] which galvanised the South African Jews. The Namaqualand Jewish community, like many other rural Jewish communities, became very involved in Zionism.[10] Herman Schapera and Joseph Galombik, particularly, were strong Zionists.

With numbers increasing, a more formal organization of the community could now be seriously considered and, in 1918, the Namaqualand Hebrew Congregation was officially formed. It was a milestone in the community's history, and showed that, even though the Jews had for many years integrated naturally with the rest of the local population, they still felt the need for some symbol of their own identity.

Springbok became the official headquarters of the widely dispersed congregation. The centre of Jewish life had moved to Springbok after the Schaperas left Garies in 1911. Boris Saharin, an immigrant from the Ukraine who arrived at about that time, had taken over the function of keeping the community together by holding religious services in his home. After him, Israel Gordon, a lawyer who settled in Springbok in 1916, had brought the Jews of the district together in Springbok to make a *minyan*.

Springbok was well on its way to becoming the capital of Namaqualand. It had survived the cessation of copper mining in 1919 because the magistracy, the Divisional Council and the police were based there. Religion, education and medicine, too, had become centralized in Springbok under the leadership of the Dutch Reformed Church's dynamic Dr W P Steenkamp.[11] In addition, Springbok was well positioned physically (reasonably accessible for most of the neighbouring towns) and the road to the north passed right through it. So, from Bitterfontein in the south to Port Nolloth in the west, congregants converged on Springbok.

The new Jewish congregation needed a home and, in

Israel Gordon in his Studebaker

Israel Gordon, lawyer, who together with his brother, Julius, was to play an important role in communal and civic life in Namaqualand, here pictured with travelling companions and his new Studebaker CBU 20, 1926.
Selina Gordon collection

Movers and Shakers

Many Jewish shopkeepers from little towns in the area are pictured in this group photograph, which, it has been suggested, may be related to the decision of the Cape Copper Company to close down the copper mines after the First World War. Protests from the Divisional Council and the local community greeted this decision and the group in this photograph may well have constituted a delegation to the mines – two Jewish lawyers are identified here. The photo is dated 1917, the year the company declared its intentions although the mines were only closed down two years later. Unfortunately the photograph cannot be formally identified as all the Cape Copper Company records were destroyed when the boat carrying them to England was torpedoed.
Sonny Josman collection

1921, was fortunate to acquire the *oude kerkie* (old little church), for its own use. Originally built as a dance hall in 1877, the building had been used since 1878 by the Dutch Reformed Church as its first place of worship in Springbok. When Dr Steenkamp arrived on the scene, he objected to church services being held in a place where there had been dancing and pressed for the building of a new church. The granite church or *klipkerk* (stone church) was duly built. The original little *kerkie* was then offered to the Jewish community and so the Namaqualand Hebrew Congregation acquired its first home.[12] Certainly, the lives of the Jewish and non-Jewish residents of Namaqualand were closely connected and everyone contributed to the formation of both communal centres. In fact, a story is told of how Dr Steenkamp went about raising money for his new church. Sidney Windisch related how the *Dominee* came to him and said 'I've put your name down on the list for

End of First World War – Peace Picnic

Peace Picnics were held across the country to celebrate the end of the First World War in 1918. Mary de Kock, daughter of Dr Michael Cowan, resident doctor at Concordia and granddaughter of the original Sylvanus Phillips of Phillips & King, recalled going to many peace picnics on Armistice Day at Modderfontein. They would go by wagon and enjoy the many sports and other events held that day. This group at the first Armistice Day celebration in Namaqualand in 1919, includes Boris Saharin, Phillip Levy and Isaac and Rose Friedlander.
Leona Perel collection

£100'. When Sidney replied '*Dominee*, I don't earn that, not for the rest of my life will I earn that', the *Dominee* replied: 'You don't have to pay it all at once, you can pay off a pound a month'!

Boris Saharin became the Reader and Jack Sovinsky the Cantor of the new congregation. Boris, after working for a while in Bowesdorp, had acquired his own shop in Springbok in 1917 and brought his nephew, Jack Sovinsky, to assist him. Jack was a young man and had trained as a choirboy in the Roeland Street synagogue in Cape Town. He had a beautiful tenor voice, so beautiful that people would gather outside the shul to listen to him sing. Jack Sovinsky, Boris Saharin and Sors Klass of Steinkopf conducted the religious services for the first official *Rosh Hashanah* held in the synagogue in 1922 and, according to Tilly Gordon, Israel's wife, the community 'was in heaven'.[13] Jews travelled from all parts of Namaqualand, mainly in Cape carts, to

Isaac Friedlander and family

Isaac Friedlander, the popular Springbok storekeeper, was unanimously voted the first President of the Namaqualand Hebrew Congregation in 1918. He came originally from Latvia, spent some years in England and was then recommended to Joseph Dembitzer in 1899 as a store assistant. He remained in Springbok for a quarter of a century. Here he is pictured outside his home in Springbok with his wife, Rose and two daughters, Queenie & Leona.
Raphael Schapera collection

Springbok Congregation

One of the earliest photographs on record of the Jewish community showing 23 men and one young boy in formal dress, dated 26 September 1919, taken by Terence McNally in Springbok. Entitled 'Springbok Congregation' it shows:
Top L-R: A Barry, L Sher, G Diamond, S Miller
4th Row L-R: W Arones, M Shapiro, I Gordon, A Levy, …
3rd Row L-R: P Levy, …, Wolman, H Klass, H Rabie, Berkowitz
2nd Row L-R: … J Ginsberg, I Friedlander, S Gordon, B Saharin, L Nainkin
Front L-R: J Sovinsky, Sher, A Sher
Bernice Spector collection

The oude kerkie

The *oude kerkie* which later became the first shul in Namaqualand, was a simple building, austere in design and constructed of rough stone with a corrugated iron roof. Tilly Gordon tells the story of how the first *Yom Kippur* celebrated in the new shul fell on a Monday, which was over *Nagmaal*. The farmers usually came in to town every three months for church services and to do their shopping. They would be in the village for three or four days, arriving on a Thursday and leaving on the following Monday or Tuesday. On this occasion, they had to wait until the fast ended and the shops reopened on Tuesday morning. Thereafter the religious leaders liased to ensure these events did not overlap. Pictured here in the foreground is Sybil Sovinsky with 'Connie' on her right.
Isobel Edelstein collection

Dr W P Steenkamp

Dr Steenkamp raising money for the new Dutch Reformed Church, the *klipkerk*, in Springbok in the early 1920s. At this point, the *oude kerkie* became available for purchase by the Jewish community as their first synagogue.
Cissie Rakoff collection

Nagmaal

Every three months farming families in the outlying district would travel to Springbok to the mother church to celebrate *Nagmaal* or Holy Communion. Here is one such family circa 1920s.
Louis van Heerde collection

Charlie Epstein outside the Garies Hotel

Charlie Epstein, one of the many bachelor clerks at the time, worked as a clerk for Abrahamson & Pachter, and is pictured here outside the Garies Hotel circa 1929.
Maxine Boyd collection

Interior of shop assistant's room

Conditions for shop assistants were not all that glamorous – many slept under the counters in the shops they served or in small back rooms. This simple room on a farm store in Bloustasie, about five miles (eight km) outside Springbok, was one of Morris Boiskin's earliest homes in Namaqualand circa 1929.
Morris Boiskin collection

celebrate the High Festivals in Springbok. Abe Schapera, Solomon Josephson and Jack Pachter did the 60 kilometres from Bowesdorp to Springbok in the record time of five hours – 'a very fast run indeed' wrote Abe Schapera, dubbing his friend, the driver of the four-horse team, 'Ben Hur Josephson'.[14]

It seems paradoxical that the Dutch Reformed Church chose to build an expensive new church and the Jews acquired their first shul at a time when there was serious drought and depression in Namaqualand. Census figures for the Jewish population do indeed show a slight dip after the war, (135 in 1918 to 113 in 1921)[15] – this was in line with general population trends. However, the core of Jewish residents had remained and been enhanced by the new professionals who came to service the developing infrastructure. Springbok was continuing to develop as an economic, health, educational and religious centre of the area. The magistrate's court had brought lawyers – Jacob Frank had come in 1907 and had left in 1917 but not before bringing Israel Gordon to Springbok in 1916 as his clerk. Israel had been articled to a legal firm in Mossel Bay and then worked for one in Cape Town. His health was not good – he had weak lungs – and when an opportunity arose

Wedding group

Wedding of Jacob Frank and Polly Barnett, daughter of Rosalia and Isaac Barnett. (Isaac was a brother of Henry Barnett who had a store in Garies).
Max Frank collection

Jacob Frank outside his offices

Jacob Frank second from right, pictured outside his office in Springbok. He was an attorney and the first Jewish professional in Namaqualand who had come to Springbok in 1907 because of the prospect of work available through the magistrate's court. He was joined by Israel Gordon in 1916 and Julius Gordon in 1918, brothers who had grown up in Riversdale and who were both lawyers. The Gordon brothers showed their commitment to Namaqualand through their involvement in civic and Jewish communal affairs for the many years they were to spend there.
Max Frank collection

to join Jacob Frank's legal practice in Namaqualand, he decided to do so because the warm, dry climate of the area would be beneficial to his health. His brother, Julius, also an attorney, joined him in 1918. The Gordon brothers, who had grown up in a small country town, Riversdale, would contribute to the vitality and development of Springbok and Namaqualand. Other professionals arrived – bookkeepers such as Charlie Epstein who worked in the Garies Hotel and teachers such as Connie Wolf and Sybil Sacks. The shopkeepers brought in more assistants or clerks.

There were many bachelors among the newcomers – young, unmarried and mischievous.[16] Dr Steenkamp was concerned about these young men and wanted them married off – he did indeed motivate for two female Jewish teachers to be appointed to the school. Sybil Sacks married Jack Sovinsky, who had his own shop by then, and told the story with relish of how she met Jack the first day after her arrival in Springbok in 1923. In her words:

> I went to Namaqualand in 1923 to teach there … Dr Steenkamp approved of my appointment because there were so many old bachelors, Israel Gordon, Julius Gordon, Ephraim Bernstine, Max Shapiro and a few others and he thought he must get one of them a wife … On the first day after my arrival, I met Jack Sovinsky and we became friendly straight away … he was a youngster of 21, the same age as me.

Clerks relaxing under a tree

Clerks from Concordia stores relaxing during their free time. L-R: Morris Boiskin with rifle, Walter Ginsberg with banjo, Samuel Kluk with record player, Solly Disner and Phillip Hirschson. *Morris Boiskin collection*

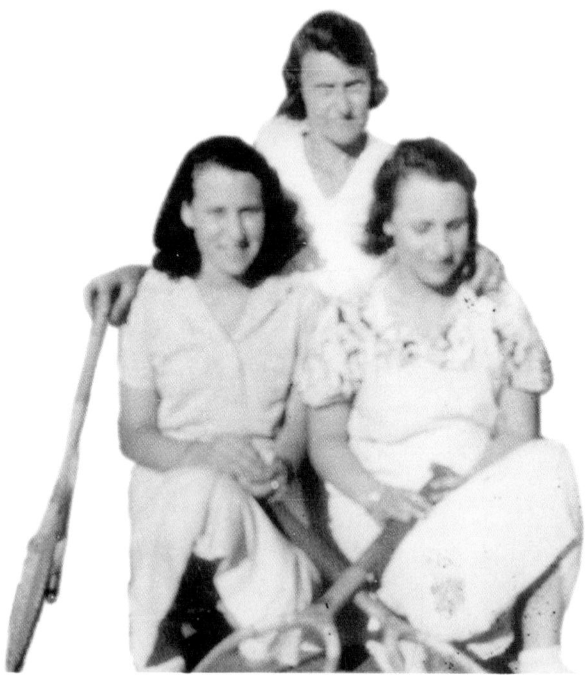

Tennis group

Namaqualand was not devoid of lively young women. Pictured here at tennis are Connie Wolf (above) and the Albert sisters, Edna and Freda, popular beauties from O'okiep. Connie later married her tennis partner, Alec Pasvolsky. *Morris Boiskin collection*

They married in 1927. So Dr Steenkamp's scheme paid off! Reminiscing years later, Sybil spoke very highly of the well-loved *Dominee* who ministered to the Dutch Reformed Church congregation in Namaqualand in the years 1919 – 1923. She was friendly with Dr Steenkamp's sister-in-law, Alice Erlank, also a teacher, and spent a lot of time at the Pastorie. The Steenkamps were very good to the young people in the village and often invited them to tea on Sunday mornings. Sybil Sovinsky must have been an entertaining teacher with her sense of humour and sporting ability – she played tennis, hockey, basketball, cricket and golf. She was not much older than the schoolgirls either. While courting Jack, a star soccer player, whom the children nicknamed 'Mak Jakkals', his soccer prowess and their relationship were the usual free-choice essay topics chosen by her pupils!

In his memoirs Abe Schapera has written numerous stories about these young men and their mischievous pranks.[17] It would seem that practical jokes were almost a way of life in the villages in those days and stories abound of the ones they played on one another. One such story involved Sors Klass, a shopkeeper in Steinkopf. He was slightly deaf and rather eccentric. Like most country storekeepers in those days, he owned two horses that were used mainly for pulling his cart. They were brown in colour and stabled near his store – during the day they roamed in the *veld* nearby. One day they wandered behind Mick Caplan's store. Mick, a notorious joker, decided to have some fun and painted one of the horses white from head to tail. The horses returned to their stables but Sors had the '*vreemde perd*'[18] sent to the pound. Luckily he discovered his mistake in time.[19]

These lively young bachelors contributed to the social life of the area. Regular Saturday night dances were held at the Concordia Club to which these eligible young men were invited. They also contributed to the cultural life of the little towns – the first syncopated dance band was started by four young men from Springbok, all of whom were Jewish: Julius Gordon, piano, Sidney Windisch, drums, Abe Schapera, banjo and Mick Farber, violin.

Sidney Windisch came to the remote area of Gamoep in Bushmanland in 1925 to relieve Max Geffen, whose wife was expecting a baby in Cape Town, and to run his shop where he traded in wool and skins. When trying to book his passage to Gamoep from Cape Town, he was told by the railway clerk 'there's no such place' and when he eventually got to Gamoep, his reaction to the only tin building which was the shop was 'Good God, Mr Geffen, I can't stay here, the bladdy lions will eat me!' He survived there for six months. After that, he moved to Steinkopf to look after Sors Klass's shop for seven months and thereafter to the Masonic Hotel in Springbok where he worked for 'Shappy' for over three years. Eventually he, too, had his own store.

As Jewish communal life became more organized, so too did Jewish involvement in local affairs. In 1921 the Jews contributed to the establishment of the first local authority, the Village Management Board. When the mines closed down in 1919, the Divisional Council requested that the Copper Company transfer the commonage to the village and recommended that a Village Management Board be established to deal with this matter. This was done and in November 1922, the first meeting of the Village Management Board was held. There were three elected members, John Hunter Roux, farmer, Israel Gordon, lawyer and Isaac Friedlander, shop-

Clerks in Concordia

Shop assistants or clerks from Concordia stores having a *le chaim* at a farewell party for one of the boys. Many of the store assistants went on to open their own stores. L-R: Morris Boiskin, Simon Murinik, Samuel Kluk, Phillip Hirshson, Alec Pasvolsky, Solly Disner, Walter Ginsberg
Morris Boiskin collection

Abe Schapera

Dapper Abe Schapera, circa 1930, was born in Garies and worked in Bowesdorp and Springbok. He played the banjo in the first syncopated dance band in Namaqualand and chronicled the life of the Jews of Namaqualand in a manuscript which he entitled 'Golden Days in Namaqualand'.

Morris Boiskin

A debonair Morris Boiskin who was now living in Concordia where he was working as shop assistant in a local store.
Morris Boiskin collection

Visit of the Earl of Athlone ▶

Official visit of the Earl of Athlone, Governor-General of the Union of South Africa and his wife, Princess Alice, granddaughter of Queen Victoria, to Namaqualand in 1926. Abe Schapera, his sister-in-law Minnie Schapera and her little daughter, Marion, formed a reception committee at the side of the main road with a bouquet of flowers put together from plants growing in paraffin tins on the stoep of the hotel at Bowesdorp. They stepped into the road, stopped the car and Marion handed over the bouquet. This photograph shows a more official reception at the Cape Copper Company offices in O'okiep, after the visitors were driven to the reception by Israel Gordon in his car CBU 20.

keeper. Roux became the first chairman. Julius Gordon was appointed secretary – at a salary of £4 per month.[20]

In addition to the legal wrangling over the transfer of the commonage, matters of sanitation and water had become urgent. The growing town (total population in 1921 of 840)[21] now had a school, a school hostel and a growing number of boys and girls in the 'indigent boarding houses', so proper sanitation arrangements had to be made. Furthermore, the boreholes were not providing sufficient water – a potential disaster in drought-prone Namaqualand where water had always been a problem. Julius Gordon wrote in 1924 'the water of the village is obtained from the fountain and is very sweet, and to this undoubtedly and its healthy altitude the village owes its clean bill of health'. After years of constant agitation the Government sent down a boring machine in the early part of 1924 and the first borehole was put down at the Residency. A strong supply of fresh water was struck at a depth of about 175 feet. (ca 54 metres) Later, water would be laid on and distributed on modern lines.[22]

Despite the lure of eligible young bachelors, a growing local population and a developing infrastructure, the fact remains that the early 1920s were essentially a time of drought and depression in Namaqualand. Yet Springbok in particular continued to develop as a centre for the Namaqualand area and the Jews continued to trickle in, providing expertise and services. They were well positioned later when a dull sparkle in the dusty earth confirmed some slow-growing rumours that had long been in the air, of a treasure-trove of diamonds deep in the heart of this barren desert.

CBU · 20

Richtersveld landscape

Looking northwards from the pinnacle of the Tatasberg, the Orange River course can be followed as it flows through some of the wildest scenery in the Richtersfeld.
Louis van Heerde collection

9 THE LURE OF DIAMONDS

The story of the discovery of diamonds in Namaqualand is integrally linked with that of Solomon Rabinowitz. He was one of the most romantic pioneers of the north-western Cape, who became known as 'King Solomon of the Richtersveld'. He came to South Africa in 1899 at the age of fifteen. Although from a religious family in Lithuania, he had always had a craving for the outdoor life and travel, and persuaded his parents to send him to South Africa.[1] He arrived just three months before the outbreak of the Anglo-Boer War and, being penniless, responded to the British Government's call for volunteers. Having 'earned some pennies', after the War ended he bought a cart, a few mules and a little stock for trading purposes and went off to Namaqualand 'into the wilds' which he loved. It was while travelling there 'among the barren mountains and the waste country desert' that he started thinking that 'God created this country for something'. It was always in his mind that there must be minerals in the area so he started picking up stones and studying them on his return home. He spent most of his money in those early days on dynamite and labour to open up holes in different places in the Richtersveld and Bushmanland, looking for copper, gold, diamonds and other minerals. One day in 1909 he received a message from Jacob Frank in Springbokfontein who had opened a legal practice in the town with a branch in Port Nolloth. A rumour had reached Frank that diamonds had been found in the vicinity of the Tatasberg in the Richtersveld near the Orange River. He and Rabinowitz formed a syndicate with a few others and Rabinowitz set out for the Richtersveld and pegged claims near what was to be Alexander Bay. Unfortunately, insufficient money was available for an extended exploration and no diamonds were discovered at that time.

Solomon Rabinowitz prospecting

Solomon Rabinowitz, one of Namaqualand's pioneering prospectors, looking for scheelite in the Richtersveld. Solomon Rabinowitz on the right, Joe Rabinowitz, a distant relative from Port Nolloth, on the left and the foreman in the centre circa 1933/34.
Joe Rabinowitz collection

Solomon married Dinah Rabinowitz, (her maiden name) also from a religious family, in 1913 and together they started a store in Port Nolloth where their first child, Gertie, was born. In 1916 they moved to Steinkopf, the Coloured mission station, where Solomon started a trading store – he was one of the first white traders to be allowed trading rights and residence there. Solomon and Dinah spent twenty years at Steinkopf and had three more children.

Solomon continued to prospect in the Richtersveld,

Interior of Solomon Rabinowitz's store in Steinkopf circa 1927

Steinkopf was a Coloured community with leadership provided by the Rhenish Missionary Society active in Namaqualand since the early 1800s. Solomon Rabinowitz's store shows shop assistants and local customers. Solomon's wife, Dinah, managed the store while he was prospecting for weeks at a time, for diamonds in the Richtersveld.
Benjamin Rabinowitz collection

Port Nolloth jetty

Two views of the jetty at Port Nolloth during its heyday as an ore port. Copper ore was transported 175 km by rail from the mines at O'okiep to Port Nolloth, from where it was shipped to Swansea, Wales. The narrow-gauge railway line ran down the jetty, allowing the ore to be loaded directly onto the waiting ships, as shown clearly in the top photo.
H.R. Moffatt collection, National Library of South Africa, Cape Town
When the copper mines closed in 1919, activity at the port decreased. This would change when diamonds were discovered there in the twenties. The railway tracks can also be seen in the lower photo, running along the jetty towards the town.
Gogh album

Diamond diggings at Alexander Bay

Many believed that diamonds originated somewhere in the interior of southern Africa and were carried down to the sea by rivers, like the Orange, where they were concentrated by wave action on to the beaches. This picture shows the terraced deposits of diamonds and fossil shells at Alexander Bay that lay under a blanket of sand, sometimes 30 feet (9 m) deep. Solomon Rabinowitz had an instinct about this and Hans Merensky, a trained geologist, recognised the fossilised oyster shells that indicated the presence of diamonds.
Cissie Rakoff collection

'a wild, desolate wasteland with a sun-tortured, ferocious landscape'[2] that fills the hook below the Orange River for its last hundred miles (160 km) to the sea. He experienced many hardships while prospecting there and nearly lost his life on a number of occasions. Once, he noticed beautiful diamond 'indications' near the mouth of the Orange River at Buchuberg but for health reasons was unable to follow up his observations. He linked up occasionally with another lone prospector, the famous Fred C Cornell. Success came finally in 1926 when Solomon found the diamonds he believed were in the Buchuberg, 40 miles (64 km) north of Port Nolloth, lying among oyster shells in diamondiferous gravel. He had followed his instinct (despite everyone laughing at him) and dug deep pits through the sand to find out if there was diamondiferous gravel underneath – he found the gravel and limestone and under that layer, a gravel bed with diamonds. The gravel bed was 'filled with fossilized oyster shells'. Solomon was an openhearted, generous man and shared everything he knew with Dr E Reuning, the agent in Namaqualand for Dr Hans Merensky, the renowned German geologist. Merensky and Reuning had been pursuing a similar line of thinking and visited Buchuberg where Solomon showed them around his trenches and the fossil oyster shells. Reuning realized that a fossilized oyster meant a pre-historic beach below the sand layers of later centuries.[3] So they 'carefully followed up and outpaced Rabinowitz' and pegged all along the fossil oyster shell line on which rich deposits of diamonds were discovered near Alexander Bay the next year. So here they were, Reuning and Merensky, twenty years after their first explorations, acquiring extensive diamond-bearing terraces very close to their original pits![4]

At the same time as Solomon found diamonds at Buchuberg and shared his discovery with Dr Merensky, a parallel story of diamond prospecting was being played out in Port Nolloth. This copper port on the west coast, approximately 100 miles (160 km) from Springbok, was a 'dead little dorp' in 1925 according to Jack Carstens, son of a local shopkeeper.[5] The town had suffered considerably after the copper mine at O'okiep closed down in 1919 because it was through the port that the ore had been shipped and the coal imported. 'Only the Jewish shops situated on a sandy strip blackened by coal dust from the wind blowing off the dumps to the south' were able to make a profit and eke out a living for themselves at that bleak time, according to Jack Carstens. 'Nothing could compete with the Jewish shopkeepers who were on their feet from early morning to late at night' he observed.

These early shopkeepers included David Rakoff, Hymie Rakoff, Herman Klass and Louis Rabinowitz (a distant relative of Solomon Rabinowitz) assisted by their wives and young Jewish clerks from the Cape. There were also the Jewish hoteliers, the Bolons, and Joseph Dembitzer's brothers, Joel and Sim.

Jack Carstens was a local boy, born in Port Nolloth in 1892, and he knew them all. His father, William, was a storekeeper in the town, and his grandfather, Captain R Carstens, had, in fact, been the Port Superintendent for the Cape Copper Company.[6] Jack grew up surrounded by the many mineral samples collected by his father, an enthusiastic amateur prospector. However, it was only after a fortune-teller in India predicted he would 'dig in the ground and find many shiny stones', that Jack become seriously interested and started following up some leads. In 1926 he did indeed pluck the first $1/2$ carat diamond from the mouth of the Kamma River six miles (nine km) south of Port Nolloth. He registered his find with the magistrate in Springbok whose response was 'For heaven's sake, don't bring me any more diamonds, they'll give me a devil of a lot of trouble', which of course they did![7]

Jack confided in his friend, Herman Klass, who was 40 years old and had been in Namaqualand for eighteen years. He had no reason to believe this dapper and well-groomed bachelor friend would be a likely candidate for roughing it in the inhospitable sands of the coast but he was wrong and, within a week of the discovery when Jack returned to the site, he discovered what diamond news meant. The whole area was pegged out and the first peg he came across was that of his friend Herman Klass. It was the signal for every Namaqualander to seek wealth in the sand, Julius Gordon said later.

In the early summer of 1926, several Jewish families who lived inland escaped to the cooler, misty climate of Port Nolloth, as was the custom, to avoid the scorching heat. Among them were the Welsh brothers Caple and Mick Caplan and Israel and Julius Gordon. Israel by this stage was a successful lawyer in Springbok and had

Alexander Bay original prospecting camp

Hymie Rakoff of Port Nolloth took this picture of the original prospecting camp of Dr Reuning who represented Dr Hans Merensky at Alexander Bay. *Cissie Rakoff collection*

become a partner with Jan Scholtz in the firm Gordon & Scholtz. The four went to explore the claims they, together with Johannes Loubser of Springbok, had pegged as a syndicate, on the northern coast of Namaqualand including the whole of Alexander Bay up to the mouth of the Orange River. With buckets and spades and lots of enthusiasm, these novices worked their claims and on the first day they found over a dozen stones.

On returning to Springbok, Israel Gordon and Jan Scholtz contacted Paul Kahn who years previously had owned a general dealer's store in Grootmis not far from the farm Kleinsee, a peaceful spot close to the mouth of the Buffels River. Farmers went there periodically to gather rushes that grew in abundance on the sandy dunes. They would use the rushes to build their *matjieshuise*, dwellings shaped liked igloos which suited the nomadic lives of the Namaqualand *trekboers*. Lime was also found in the surroundings of Grootmis and, at that time, was being used for whitewashing the walls of the new schoolhouse being built there. The lime was cleaned of clay and other substances before use, but in the process thousands of pounds worth of diamonds clinging to the clay were unwittingly thrown away. The builder of the school, a Mr Alberts, was also a casual prospector and had noticed a glittering object in the sand. He also happened to be the brother-in-law of one of the syndicate members, Jan Scholtz.[8] In no time at all, 'Oom Paul' Kahn, who still owned a piece of this 'worthless' farming land, and some other farmers had been persuaded to sell their land to the syndicate. Within a month, 600 carats of diamonds had been found worth about £6 000 and thereafter, option hunters descended on the area, amongst them Dr Hans Merensky.

Merensky bought up the claims of Solomon Rabinowitz and the Jewish syndicates (not without some whisky and soda to nudge the process along) paying the Gordon syndicate members what was considered good money in those days – £17 500.[9] The Gordon syndicate members were Israel and Julius Gordon, Caple Caplan and Daniel Loubser. Caple Caplan tossed in his single claim 'as a Christmas present' and in fact it was this claim that produced the perfect blue-white 85 carat diamond, the prize among the 12 420 carats of diamonds valued at £154 000 produced by Merensky's group by January 1927. Florrie Caplan, Caple's wife remained quite bitter about her husband's thoughtless generosity although Merensky sent gifts to the families every year and Florrie and her sister, Yetta, married to Mick Caplan, received a gift of diamonds from him. Caple started building a second hotel in Springbok with the money he received from the sale – the Springbok Hotel – and the Gordons put some of their money into Namaqua House, built in 1929, and today a landmark in Burg Street, Cape Town.

Merensky realized the implications of a deluge of gems on to the international market – it could flood the market with great quantities of exceptional quality gems and the bottom could fall out of the market. The situation was exacerbated by the discovery of more exceptional quality diamonds at Lichtenberg in the Transvaal in 1926, and Merensky persuaded the Government to intervene and the Precious Stones Bill was initiated. Until it was passed no mining could take place in the region. Months went by while the Bill was debated and amended. In the meantime, Namaqualanders waited for the outcome, and vast areas of Namaqualand continued to lie idle. The pegged areas and farms were deserted. Another year's crops failed. The situation became so serious that a deputation of diggers went twice to Pretoria to meet with the Minister of Mines with a list of proposals which could provide reasonable opportunities for the local diggers and, at the same time, enable the government to control the output.[10]

Namaqua House

Namaqua House in Burg Street, Cape Town was built by the Gordon brothers from the proceeds of the sale of their shares in the diamond syndicate to Hans Merensky. Built in 1929, the building is a fine example of art deco architecture and is a landmark in the city today.
Charles Maggs

The Precious Stones Act was finally passed in November 1927. It prohibited any body corporate, which did not hold claims or diggers certificates before 1 July of the previous year, from exercising any rights in the area through subsequent investment. It restricted the number of persons who could be employed to work

Diamonds

This postcard shows the 25,760 carats of diamonds taken out in one day at Hans Merensky's camp at Alexander Bay on 17 May 1929. Compared with the tiny diamonds in these earrings which were a gift to Florrie Caplan from Hans Merensky, it is small wonder that Florrie was bitter at her husband Caple's generosity in giving away what proved to be the richest claim in the area.
Joe Rabinowitz collection
Maureen Miller collection

one claim to 20 persons. Soon after, the State itself became a 'landlord of important mining property' and established the State Alluvial Diggings at Alexander Bay. Jack Carstens was appointed Mine Superintendent at Kleinsee and placed in charge of all mining operations. He was destined to spend thirty years in all among the diamonds of Kleinsee.[11]

But trouble was brewing. Poor Namaqualand farmers south of Port Nolloth had given options to syndicates to mine on their land and in return had received a monthly rental. The Government withdrew permission for this arrangement in October 1928 and decided that farmers had to prospect and mine themselves and then only if their farm was free of debt. Of course no farmer was free of debt, crops had failed and the desperately

Manie Maritz

Manie Maritz addresses a gathering of diamond diggers in Port Nolloth at the time of the diggers' rebellion in 1929.
Cissie Rakoff collection

needed monthly rent was now no longer forthcoming. Farmers were forced off their farms and sought work in Port Nolloth. At the same time, diamond diggers from Lichtenburg in the Transvaal were descending on the town despite warnings about the deteriorating conditions and lack of opportunities. The locals resented their arrival and by December the Namaqualanders decided to take matters into their own hands and take Alexander Bay by force. So there were two battles in progress – the Namaqualanders against the Government and the Namaqualanders against the Lichtenburgers. By the beginning of 1929 the stage was set for a siege of the State Diggings and at one of the meetings, held at Sim Dembitzer's Commercial Hotel, Manie Maritz arrived. He was the idol of Namaqualand after his exploits in the Anglo-Boer War, and he, too, had a vested interest in the diggings as he had pegged a claim in the area. Maritz urged caution and discretion and instead of a rebellion, a committee was appointed to meet the Minister of Mines. The Government thereupon appointed Maritz as Welfare Officer for the Distressed Portions of Namaqualand. But there was still no relief for the plight of the poor Namaqualander during the drought and depression.[12]

As for the prospectors, Rabinowitz summed up his lot in his biography: 'to fight nature, single-handed in the desert without water, without money and without sympathy from anyone … a man must have an iron will to stick it out but thank God, I succeeded and I think Namaqualand will be in the future one of the richest

Camel patrol

Camel patrols were used to protect the diamond fields.
Raphael Schapera collection

mineral districts in SA especially in the Richtersveld where I personally came across rich deposits of copper, diamonds, gold, bismuth, mica, beryl, lithium-mica, corundum, titanite, columbite, galena and scheelite ...'[13] Rabinowitz hoped to see all Namaqualanders alike make a comfortable living from the area's rich mineral deposits. 'I love Namaqualand', he is quoted as saying 'and nothing would please me more than that my children should be able to say, My father did something for Namaqualand'.[14]

Neither he, Fred Cornell nor Jack Carstens benefited from their finds – in fact, Cornell had been looking for the reputed mountain of gold in the Richtersveld, but found diamonds instead. In 1921 he was killed in a freak motor-cycle accident in London where he was trying to raise the capital to exploit his find. The Namaqualanders, according to Ellis Caplan '*het bogger all gekry*'[15] and thus began the inevitable sequel to the story: illicit diamond buying or IDB as it was called.

For poverty-stricken Namaqualanders, the temptation to deal in diamonds was irresistible, especially in the early days when patrolling was non-existent and, in any event, they felt it was their right. Stories abound of those IDB days. Port Nolloth's two hotels became known as the IDB hotel and the CID hotel. Residents of the little *dorps* at that time, such as Mina Gomes, Paul Kahn's daughter in Komaggas, remember the activity in the dead of night – the sound of cars making quick getaways with the police in hot pursuit. Arthur Rosenberg, son of Max Rosenberg of Garies, remembers his father telling him of the cars that used to pass at high speed through Garies at night. Shappy's nephew, Solly Grod, whom Shappy fetched to help him in the hotel during the diamond boom because he could not cope with the 'thousands' of people who wanted accommodation, tells how they sold petrol from the pumps in the middle of the night.

There was no end to the innovative ways in which people attempted to smuggle diamonds out of the mines in Namaqualand: buying motor cars and exiting the garages via the back to escape the police waiting in the front; landing on the coast by light aircraft to pick up a packet of diamonds thrown over the security fence only to be bogged down in the sand when the tide came in; diamonds being stuffed into tubes of toothpaste and so on. Simon Jowell, who came to live in Springbok some years later and practiced as an attorney, was the defence lawyer for a group of men who got caught in the 'Veggat' incident. The prospectors believed that diamonds rumoured to be in a hole centimetres deep near Port Nolloth, belonged to them and they were determined to take the diamonds. The police got there first and formed a ring around the hole. The prospectors encircled the police but when the first shot was fired, they ran away. Three were caught and tried in the Port Nolloth Magistrate's Court. During a recess in the trial, two people sitting at the back in heavy coats and dark glasses (it was mid summer in Namaqualand!) approached Simon Jowell and asked if he would get them off. Wanting to know what their interest was, they replied they were two who had got away.

A famous diamond theft was the Bitterfontein train robbery in 1931. The monthly diamond production from the Kleinsee diggings was driven by car to Springbok by the mine manager accompanied by a police escort. Astonishingly, these stones would then be weighed and counted in the public office of the magistrate's court in full view of anyone wishing to be present. They would then be parceled up, sealed and posted at the Springbok Post Office, to be mailed to Cape Town via Bitterfontein.

On this occasion the parcel containing 10 000 carats and valued at £53 000 arrived at Bitterfontein to await the Cape Town train. It was delivered to the post office at the station, an edifice described by Carstens as a 'tin shanty' with a door secured by a lock so flimsy, that it offered no resistance to anyone planning to break in.[16] The next morning there was no sign of the parcel of diamonds – only a gaping hole in the corrugated iron wall of the post office.[17] Two men were eventually arrested and tried for the theft. On apprehending them, police found 3 000 carats of diamonds which served as evidence. However, nimble defence on the part of their lawyer cast doubt on the source of the stones and persuaded the judge to deliver a verdict of 'not guilty'. Thus some 7 000 carats of the stolen Kleinsee diamonds made their way into the main stream of illicit diamond dealing.

The discovery of diamonds at Alexander Bay in 1927 brought a new lease of life, albeit short-lived, to Namaqualand. Certainly, the profile of the area was raised considerably and local business flourished.

'Blitspatrolie' by the Alexander Bay diamond police

Groups of young police graduates were sent straight from college to Alexander Bay to help secure the diamond mine. The uniforms worn by some of the men in this picture are those of the Alexander Bay diamond police.
Louis van Heerde collection

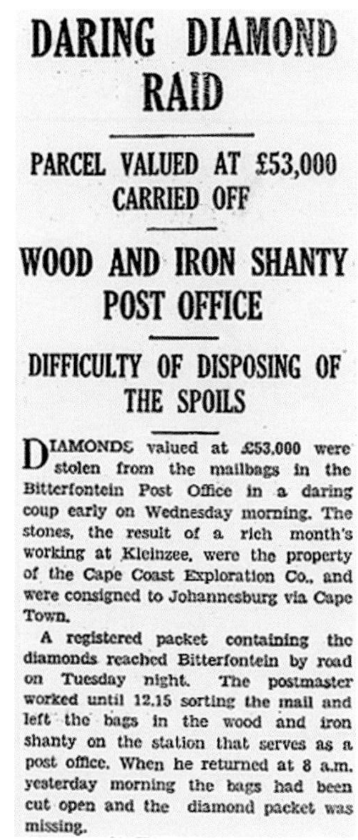

DARING DIAMOND RAID

PARCEL VALUED AT £53,000 CARRIED OFF

WOOD AND IRON SHANTY POST OFFICE

DIFFICULTY OF DISPOSING OF THE SPOILS

DIAMONDS valued at £53,000 were stolen from the mailbags in the Bitterfontein Post Office in a daring coup early on Wednesday morning. The stones, the result of a rich month's working at Kleinzee, were the property of the Cape Coast Exploration Co., and were consigned to Johannesburg via Cape Town.

A registered packet containing the diamonds reached Bitterfontein by road on Tuesday night. The postmaster worked until 12.15 sorting the mail and left the bags in the wood and iron shanty on the station that serves as a post office. When he returned at 8 a.m. yesterday morning the bags had been cut open and the diamond packet was missing.

J.D. du PLESSIS & COMPANY
PRIVATE HOTEL
& CAFE

10 LOTS TO CELEBRATE

During the 1930s the Jewish community in Namaqualand enjoyed what came to be known as their 'Golden Age'. This was in sharp contrast to the rest of the country, and indeed the Western world, which was suffering from a severe economic depression in the aftermath of the 1929 New York Stock Market collapse.

Business in Namaqualand generally had profited from the discovery of diamonds in 1927. The hotels were filled to capacity; the building industry boomed and houses sprang up; shopkeepers benefited as business flowed in. Motoring became Namaqualand's newest industry: it brought fresh faces to Namaqualand – amongst them, Solomon Kluk of Garies and Joseph Jowell of Springbok. The motor car, 'this iron and petrol thing',[1] caught the imagination of the farmers and their sons who soon started deserting the farms for the *dorps* to be trained as motor mechanics in the motor garages and workshops springing up all over. Petrol was in great demand and many shopkeepers, like the Levy brothers in Springbok, installed pumps outside their stores. Solomon Kluk and his father came to South Africa from Poland in 1920, and both worked for a while in concession stores in Concordia, until Solomon bought his own business in Garies and started selling second-hand cars.

Springbok was particularly well placed to take advantage of the boom because of its location on the transport route and its developing infrastructure and service industry. Its development as a commercial centre had been boosted by the discovery of diamonds. By 1929, its population stood at 2 000 persons (approximately the same as at the height of the copper mining mania in 1865) out of a total population for Namaqualand which two years later stood at 23 353.[2]

Selling petrol

Everyone was pumping petrol during the diamond boom. Here Alfred and Phillip Levy, shopkeepers, are standing at the Pegasus pumps outside Phillip Levy's store in Springbok in 1929. Over the years 'Levy Brothers' (Phillip, Alfred and Charles) developed branches in O'okiep, Nababeep, Concordia, Springbok, Vioolsdrift and Port Nolloth. Their father, Maurice Levy, came to Namaqualand after the Boer War and had opened the original shop in Nababeep.

◀ **J D du Plessis & Co**

The business of J D du Plessis & Co, later to become Jowells Garage, seen from the koppie in the centre of the village in 1934.

Frank Kitto prospecting in the veld

Frank Kitto is pictured here alongside the Cape Copper Company cart while prospecting in Carolusberg. At the mine shaft on the right is one of his two daughters, Betty, wearing a white hat. *Betty Wright collection*

Adding to the general mood of optimism was the announcement early in October 1929 of the imminent re-opening of the copper mine at O'okiep. Despite the fact that the copper mines had closed down after the First World War, they had been maintained and prospecting for copper had continued. A skeleton staff had remained at the mines headed in the 1920s by Frank Kitto, a Cornishman. Many of the miners were descendants of the original Cornishmen who had come out in the mid-1850s when copper mining began. William Kitto, Frank's grandfather, came to Namaqualand as a general manager of the Cape Copper Company in 1881. Frank came out in 1914 also as manager, and lived in the O'okiep Grange, which had been built for his grandfather. An American company, calling itself the South African Copper Company, had decided to take up its three-year option on the O'okiep mine and had sunk a new shaft and opened an assay office on the site. Copper exploration was starting up again.

At this time, it is estimated that the Jewish population of the area had swelled to 200 persons[3] (from 115 in 1926).[4] The bachelors had settled down and started families so there were many more women and children. Provision for women worshippers in almost all the early synagogues in the country was totally inadequate. The Namaqualand Hebrew Congregation was no exception and had to make changes.[5] By 1929 the shul committee felt it was time to construct a new synagogue in order both to accommodate the women and to have a building that was more prestigious in appearance and befitting of the new status of the Jewish community. The building committee comprised David Gelb, Herman Klass, Israel Gordon and Ephraim Bernstine, a Springbok shopkeeper. Tenders went out for the new shul and M Klawansky of Krugersdorp was awarded the contract for the building of the new synagogue – his tender was for £3 724. Klawansky had built the new municipal buildings in Springbok after the discovery of diamonds, or, as Sybil Sovinsky said years later, 'when Springbok became a metropolis on account of the diamonds'.

The acquisition of a site for the building of a synagogue involved dealings with the Copper Company. Transfer of land was a problem unresolved from the time when the public village had been created by Phillips & King in the previous century – a problem with which the Village Management Board of Springbok was still grappling and which usually involved long delays and legal wrangling. However, Frank Kitto, the manager of the mine, was well disposed to the Jewish community which was very lucky for them because the transfer of the ground adjoining the old shul site on which the Jewish community now wished to develop a new shul, might have taken a long time to negotiate but, instead, was readily and graciously granted by Kitto.

A building fund was established and members of the congregation, businessmen and other locals were asked to contribute through levies and donations. Fundraising events were organized. Jews and non-Jews were approached, as were companies in Cape Town who did business with Springbok. A loan, secured by a bond, was obtained in Cape Town. David Gelb gave up much of his personal time to fundraise. Raphael Gelb, his son, later said his father neglected his business (the shop and mill in Concordia) to go around collecting for the new shul and that he spent three months calling on every wholesaler, Jewish and non-Jewish, who had Jewish customers in Namaqualand.

David Gelb, Max Shapiro, Israel Gordon and Caple Caplan made up the deputation that set off for Cape Town to raise money. They reported that they were 'received most courteously by all the firms with one exception – J W Jagger & Co'. Jaggers, as the company was known, was one of the Cape Town wholesale firms which regularly supplied country stores through their commercial travellers all the way up the west coast. Mr Jagger had received them in person but was 'insulting and abusive'.[6]

The deputation returned to Namaqualand but along the way instituted a boycott of Jaggers among storekeepers all the way from Cape Town to Springbok. It was not long before Jaggers' traveller called on Mr Bernstine, the Secretary of the Congregation, with a cheque for £25 and tendered Mr Jagger's apology. The Committee

Tennis group

Lively social gathering for tennis at the Kitto home in O'okiep, 1931. Seemingly all the young people enjoyed playing social tennis. Top L-R: Madge Nel (Doris Jowell's sister), George Aschman, visiting journalist, Betty Kitto (Frank Kitto's daughter) and Milly Saharin, elegant as always, sitting in front between Joan Kitto (another daughter) on the left and an unidentified visitor on the right.
Saharin collection

The old and new synagogues

The pride of the Namaqualand Hebrew Congregation - the new synagogue, framed by pepper trees and situated alongside its predecessor. The Cape Copper Company gave its approval for the use of the ground and in April 1929, Mr M Klawansky's building tender was accepted and the first concrete poured The foundation stone was laid in July and in September the Jewish community celebrated its first *Rosh Hashanah* in the new synagogue.

Interior of the new shul

The original furnishings were an informal collection of chairs and benches, probably from the old synagogue. It was only after Raphael, David Gelb's son, came home after the Second World War and became secretary of the synagogue, that he realised his vision for a more formal furnishing of the interior as shown in this photograph.

Jack Sovinsky, cantor, Mayoral Sunday 1961

regarded this as a greater insult 'because it appears your firm considers that it can buy this community'. They volunteered to make good to the Congregation the £25, returned Jagger's cheque and demanded a letter of apology before any donation would be accepted and the boycott (or 'present attitude') lifted. Jagger relented, wrote a full apology, sent his cheque of £25 and 'the boycott was withdrawn'. Copies of the apology were circulated among the local Jewry.[7]

The building of the new synagogue was underway and such was the goodwill between the community and their non-Jewish neighbours in those years, that invitations to the laying of the foundation stone were sent out in the form of a public announcement to each village – O'okiep, Port Nolloth, Steinkopf, Concordia, Klawer and Garies – inviting their residents to the celebrations. On June 1929, David Gelb laid the foundation stone of the new shul. He succeeded Isaac Friedlander as President of the Namaqualand Hebrew Congregation.

Members of other local denominations attended the consecration of the new synagogue – Dr W L Steenkamp was present accompanied by some other dignitaries of the Dutch Reformed Church. The local Anglican minister was also present. A dance was organized for that evening to celebrate the event and to raise funds. Donations of money as well as donations in kind were received – a local farmer donated 10 sheep for the dance.

The shul was completed in time for the High Festivals that year and on 4 October 1929 – the first day of *Rosh Hashanah* – the synagogue was officially opened. The synagogue was built only ten years after the founding of the Congregation, an amazing achievement especially considering that the post-war depression in South Africa had lasted for three of those years – from roughly 1920 to 1923. The old shul continued to be used as a communal hall.

The Jewish community in the 1930s was an active, dynamic, and, like many other Jewish bodies, volatile one with many differences of opinion. But the commun-

David Gelb

A studio portrait of David Gelb, shopkeeper in Concordia and later Springbok, who was to play an important role in Jewish communal life.
Raphael and Thelma Gelb collection

Celebrating Rosh Hashanah in 1930

Identifiable in the group celebrating *Rosh Hashanah* were – back row L-R: Morris Milner, Naomi Diamond, Mr Weisman and Mr Reich (with cigarette) and front row L-R: Miss Diamond, Alec Pasvolsky, Sidney Windisch (centre), Miss Diamond to his left and one of the Simon brothers on the right.
Morris Boiskin collection

ity remained cohesive. They were fiercely independent and brooked no interference from the Cape Jewish Board of Deputies and Beth Din (Jewish Ecclesiastical Court) whose emissaries would be sent packing back to the Cape if no prior arrangements for meeting them had been made. They had the utmost confidence in their own ability and resources to perform religious and other rites.

Interesting newcomers in the early 1930s were the Abramson brothers. Harry and Abraham were jewellers. Harry, in typical Namaqualand nicknaming style, was known as 'long Abramson' and Abraham as 'short Abramson'. The brothers had trained as jewellers in St Petersburg – home of Fabergé. They set up independent jewellery stores in Springbok. Two sons were born to Harry and Ella, Aubrey in 1939 and Mark in 1942. Abraham and Fanny also had two sons, Max and Sam.

There were *brises*, *barmitzvahs* and weddings with or without their own minister. Victor Caplan, son of Caple and Florrie, and Harold Gelb, son of David & Millie, had celebrated their *barmitzvahs* in the old shul early in 1929 but Ellis Caplan, Victor's brother, and Ivan and Raphael Gelb, Harold's younger brothers, celebrated theirs in the new shul. The Gelb boys were taught their portions of the law by the Kluks (father Moses, and two sons, Solomon and Samuel, who had come from Bialystok in Poland in about 1920 and worked for David Gelb) and Ellis was taught his *parsha* by Sammy Berkowitz, the *shammash* (beadle). Sammy was loved by the children because he was 'one of those old-time philosophers, his broken English and broken Afrikaans and his Yiddish and Polish, they were all mixed up together. And of course, the wonderful ginger beer he made – that was the main attraction!'- reminisced Ellis

Caplan many years later. The first wedding in the shul took place in June 1935 when Sidney Windisch married Naomi Diamond, a local girl. The Reverend Solomon Berelowitz, Bessie Jowell's father, had to travel 250 miles (400 km) from Calvinia to officiate because, as yet, there was no resident minister. It was the first Jewish wedding in Namaqualand and, as a gift, the congregation gave the couple free use of the shul.[8]

By 1935 there was a new generation of young children growing up who needed a Jewish education. So the post was advertised and in July 1936 (in that year, official census figures show 116 Jews in Namaqualand) the first minister was appointed – the Rev Segal who fulfilled the function of religious leader, *chazzan*, *schochet* and teacher. He was engaged at £25 per month plus a 2 lb (0.9 kg) meat allowance daily and £2 10 shillings extra for teaching in Garies twice a month. In Springbok, *cheder* classes were held in the shul hall. *Kosher* meat became available in Namaqualand for the

Namaqualand sport

Sport was introduced into Namaqualand by the immigrant Cornish miners who came to work on the copper mines in the latter half of the nineteenth century. They brought with them the traditional English games – cricket, golf, soccer, rugby and tennis.

A cricket event at Garies in the early 1930s which includes Max Rosenberg in large straw hat (top row 3rd left) and Jack Pachter (bottom row 2nd right). After Joseph Dembitzer left Springbok, he donated a major cricket trophy, the Dembitzer Cricket Cup.
Maxine Boyd collection

Soccer was popular among the young men. The Springbok Association Football Club Minute Book reveals Jewish involvement from the first meeting in April 1914 where Jacob Frank and Isaac Friedlander are recorded as founder members. Later members included Herman Klass, Boris Saharin, Ephraim Bernstine, E Wolf, Solomon Josephson, Jack Pachter and Jack Sovinsky (who was unanimously elected captain of the club in 1921).

The photograph below shows the Garies team in the early 1930s and includes Max Rosenberg (top 2nd left) and Jack Pachter (bottom 2nd left) with their team-mates.
Jack Pachter collection

Sunday afternoon picnic

Sunday afternoon picnics were a feature of life in Namaqualand. So many remembered the happy Sundays spent picnicking in the veld. Included in this group of picnickers are Doris Jowell (Simon Jowell's wife), top left, Ellis Caplan, front middle and Simon Jowell (Joseph Jowell's brother) bottom right. Circa 1937.
Ellis Caplan collection

Friends

Life for the children. A 'wonderful childhood' said Pauline Saharin, daughter of Boris and Milly, pictured here with playmates Regie, Lynton & Merle Rabie, the children of the Barclays Bank manager and his wife, Lulu.
Saharin collection

Birthday girl

Pauline Saharin, dressed for her party on her parents' trellised stoep, Springbok, sporting her birthday gift of a new watch, circa 1937.
Saharin collection

first time. Rev Segal ministered to the congregation until 1939 and during that time there was another wedding, a double wedding – Naomi Windisch's brother, Zalman Diamond married May Kelman and her sister, Becky Diamond married Solly Kelman. There was also a *barmitzvah*, that of Benjy Rabinowitz, son of Dinah and Solomon Rabinowitz. Benjy recalls the 'big do' the community had for him after the service, catered by the Namaqualand Women's Zionist Society.

There was a group of active young women by then, including Tilly Gordon, Sybil Sovinsky, Bessie Jowell and Milly Saharin, and women's activities generally took a new form. The Namaqualand Women's Zionist Society was established early in the 1930s, preceding by some years membership rights of women to the Namaqualand Hebrew Congregation. Women were first allowed to attend the Annual General Meeting of the Congregation in 1932 and only in 1935, after three years of debate, were they finally admitted to its membership – and then, with a proviso that 'a lady shall not be eligible for posts of chairman, vice-chairman, treasurer or secretary' and further that the nominal subscription of five shillings and three pence be payable in advance! At that momentous annual general meeting of 7 October 1935, 36 women were accepted as members. (White South African women had obtained the vote in 1930). Most meetings of the Congregation were held in the old shul building.

Once accepted, the women became increasingly important in the communal life of the congregation, particularly in the sphere of fundraising. Finances were always an important issue in the community – the funding of the new shul, its maintenance and furbishing etc – and they were often in overdraft at the bank. When the Women's Zionist Society was formed, the men's committee hoped this would be an avenue for collecting

First wedding

The first wedding in the new shul, the marriage of Naomi Diamond to Sidney Windisch, 1935. Amongst the wedding party from L-R: Joe Jowell, Milly Saharin (back, with large-brimmed hat), Pauline Saharin (flower girl, front left), and the bride and groom, Naomi (*née* Diamond) and Sidney Windisch on the right.
Sidney Windisch collection

Morning Tea

Welcome tea for a newcomer. Ettie, wife of Abe Schapera, newly arrived in Springbok, 1930, at morning tea in the Saharin house in Springbok. From L-R: Ettie Schapera, Doreen Sovinsky (elder child of Jack and Sybil), Milly and Boris Saharin.
Saharin collection

In front of Masonic Hotel

Sybil Sovinsky and Bessie Jowell in front of Shappy's Masonic Hotel attending a farewell party for a friend circa 1930.
Betty Wright collection

Springbok in the 30s ▶

A crocodile in Springbok? This picture shows children crossing the main street on their way from the school hostel to church one Sunday morning in 1930. Springbok, by that time, had become the centre of Namaqualand in the fields of religion, medicine, social welfare, commerce and education. The town's population had reached 2 000 people at the beginning of the 1930s. Modern education had arrived with the appointment of Pieter ('Oom Piet') van Heerde as head of the Secondary School at Springbok in 1926, and within two years of his appointment he had established a high school. The school itself dated back to 1905, and the first attendance register of that year showed 14 children enrolled.
Ellis Caplan collection

revenue – which indeed it became, and once women sat on the shul committee, even more so. In 1937 the ladies' society contributed £63 towards the £80 needed for electrical installation. There were sufficient funds to replace Rev Segal after he left and to engage the Rev G Gad, who ministered to the congregation until 1942.

The women held two functions a year. One was a social event, usually a picnic on a farm outside Springbok to celebrate *Yom Ha'atzmaut* – the anniversary of the establishment of the State of Israel. The other was a fund-raising Zionist Ball which became a highlight in the social life of Springbok. Thelma Gelb, wife of Raphael, recalls selling tickets for the Ball on the streets of Springbok – '*kaartjies vir ons kerk*'[9] and being told '*Ag, Mevrou, ons sal 'n kaartjie koop, ons dans mos nie, maar ons kom lekker eet*'.[10] In reminiscing about the Zionist Balls, Sybil Sovinsky remembered some of the menus – 'out of this world' they were, usually consisting of potato salad, chopped liver, turkey, coq au vin, occasionally spaghetti bolognaise – all hot meat and cold salads. Sybil herself was an outstanding cook and baked beautifully; she often walked off with the prizes at the Vroue Landbou Vereniging.[11] Local bands provided the music in the early years.

Although the Jewish community in Namaqualand expanded during their 'Golden Age' of the thirties, the local farming community was suffering from drought and the effects of the Great Depression of 1931-32. The stage was being set for one of the darkest periods in world history and another world war was looming.

GRINDING POVERTY IN THE NORTH-WEST CAPE

FORMER WELL-TO-DO FARMERS' VAIN SEARCH FOR WORK

STEALING TO SAVE FAMILY FROM STARVATION

POSITION AGGRAVATED BY DISMISSAL OF 250 LABOURERS

THE dismissal of 250 men, 60 of them Europeans, on account of the completion of the Olifant's River irrigation scheme, has once more drawn attention to the grave distress which prevails among the once prosperous farming community in the North-West Cape.

Striking examples of this are given in the interview below with Dr. Steenkamp, M.P. for Namaqualand, whose postbag daily reveals many tragedies of poverty and misery.

One of the doctor's correspondents this week stated bluntly that, after tramping hundreds of miles in search of work, he had been forced to steal to save his wife and children from starvation. Another, because he is unable to raise £86 arrears interest on a £2,000 bond, has been forced to throw his farms, valued at £7,000, on the market.

TRAGEDIES IN DR. STEENKAMP'S POSTBAG

11 DARKER TIMES

'Grinding poverty in the North West Cape'. This headline from the *Cape Argus* of 19 April 1930 aptly sums up the situation in Namaqualand during the early 1930s. Repercussions of the dramatic collapse of the New York Stock Exchange in October 1929, combined with one of the severest droughts of the twentieth century, as well as a slump in the copper and diamond mining industries led to severe economic problems for the local communities.

Destitute young Jews again started arriving in Namaqualand looking for work but there was none – the local Jews helped them with some money and sent them on their way.

The generosity of the local Jews also extended to non-Jews. The shopkeepers and hoteliers again helped tide farmers over the difficult years – one of the severest droughts of the century hit the Cape region during 1932-33. Theunis Uys recalls his youth in Port Nolloth and describes how the Jewish shopkeepers always helped them with '*'n paar sjielings kontant om darem kerkgeld te hê*'[1] and how David Rakoff extended credit to Theunis' mother and always gave her '*'n kardoesie lekkers as pasella*'[2] when she came into the shop to pay off her debts. Theunis writes of 'Oom Paul' Kahn of Komaggas and of Shappy of the Masonic Hotel, Springbok, both of whom helped the Coloured people during those years. 'Oubaas Solly' – Solomon Rabinowitz of Steinkopf, too, is remembered by many of the old Coloured people in the area as '*'n baie goeie mens*'[3] who helped them. Theunis writes of Rabinowitz in his unpublished manuscript: '*Hy het hulle deur moeilike tye met voorskootte gedra en meer as sy deel gedoen vir die armes en behoeftige van sy ongewing*'.[4] He was referring to the Coloured people of the Richtersveld and Steinkopf. Dave Teperson, who grew up in Garies where his parents ran the Garies Hotel which they bought from the Rosenbergs in 1941/42, states emphatically that 'Jewish shops kept the farmers alive' by giving them extensive credit.[5]

First-hand evidence of this, during a drought in the twenties, is provided by the bookkeeper of Sors Klass in Steinkopf, in this letter to merchants found among Sors' papers:

> Dear Sirs,
> You ask me for money to pay my account. But do you know that we have a drought? Do you know that there is no harvest? Do you know that the sheep are dying? Do you know that the farmers are going bankrupt? Do you know that we must still help the farmers? Well, I know that you don't know, or you would not ask me for money which I haven't got. Anyhow I don't blame you for trying. But don't worry, if I don't pay you then God will pay you.
>
> Good-bye and Good luck,
> Yours truly
> Sors Klass

– and that from a man who was fluent in Afrikaans and Yiddish, as were most *Boere Jode* at that time, but not good at English![6]

It is not surprising, therefore, that there was a rapport between the Jews and the Afrikaners in Namaqualand. First the *smous*, and later the shopkeepers and hoteliers provided an economic service to the local inhabitants and together they struggled through

◀ Waiting for rations

Part of the crowd in Garies waiting to receive 'pauper' rations during the depression years.
The rations consisted of 7 lbs (3kg) of wheat per week per adult.
Maxine Boyd collection

Drought relief

Essential foods were donated and distributed to the stricken areas by truck during the depression and drought years. This picture shows a truck offloading tinned foods, cocoa, coffee and other necessities to a local store in Garies.
Rosenberg family collection

Lulu Rabie circa 1946

Louise Marie (known as Lulu) Rabie, wife of the Barclays Bank manager, Eric Rabie, formed warm friendships with her Jewish neighbours. Her interest in Jewish customs earned her the title of 'The best Jewess in the North Western Cape'.
Merle Rabie collection

and survived the hard times. The Dutch Reformed Church chronicler writes '*immers, in geen ander distrik het daar nog altyd so 'n hartelike verhouding tussen die Joodse gemeenskap en die christelike samelewing bestaan as in hierdie land nie*'.[7] The DRC ministers took to checking their calendar with the Jewish calendar when planning *Nagmaal* services to ensure that *Nagmaal* did not clash with the Jewish High Festivals and that the Jewish shops would be open during those occasions, four times a year, when the farmers came to town.[8]

Close friendships were forged – Lulu Rabie, wife of the manager of Barclays Bank, became very friendly with the Jewish women particularly Milly Saharin, Bessie Jowell and Millie Gelb; and her children became good friends with the Gordon and Saharin children. (Millie and David Gelb and their family had moved to Springbok in 1933. David Gelb had actually sold his business in Concordia in 1930 but then, when news of the mine closing down reached him in 1931, he telegraphed the new owner to inform him and the deal was cancelled – typical of the honourable way in which he conducted his life.) Lulu sang at concerts, accompanied by Milly at the piano. Both women were accomplished performers. Lulu joined the Namaqualand Women's Zionist Organization, fasted on the Day of Atonement because all her friends fasted and anyway she thought it was a 'good, healthy idea', and was dubbed 'The Best Jewess in the North Western Cape'. There were other close friendships: Bessie Jowell, Marian van Niekerk, wife of the district surgeon and Helen van Heerde, wife of the principal of the high school, became close friends. All three were involved in organizing assistance for the poor during the depression years and all three played a leading role in the development of the community in Springbok. Lulu Rabie said: 'There was always a mutual understanding between the Jewish and non-Jewish inhabitants of Namaqualand. We all helped and stood by one another'.

Business partnerships between Jews and non-Jews developed. Israel Gordon was in partnership with Jan Scholtz in a legal firm, and Joe Jowell was in a motor business with Jaap du Plessis. Joe Jowell had come to Namaqualand in April 1929. He was a qualified lawyer but his poor eyesight (he has lost most of the sight of his right eye as a result of trachoma as a child in Riebeeck West and only had 40% vision in his left eye) took much strain during his years of study and legal practice and he developed migraine headaches. He gave up law and took over the Chevrolet sub-agency for the Namaqualand region from Calvinia Motors, the business belonging to his future brother-in-law, Benjamin Berelowitz. Joe married Rebecca Berelowitz, affectionately known as Bessie (she couldn't pronounce her r's so in fact it was her preference) in Calvinia, in September that year and

Joseph and Rebecca Jowell

A young Joe and Bessie Jowell, in carefree pose with friend Sarah Braude from Riebeeck West, Joe's home town.

Plaatjie

Plaatjie, the makeshift truck built by Joe Jowell and his partner Jaap du Plessis in 1930. It was made from an old Buick motor car and parts of a 1 $^{1}/_{2}$ ton Chevrolet truck, and heralded the start of the Jowell Transport business.

First Threshing Machine in Namaqualand

Wheat was still being produced in the Namaqualand in the 1920s. Arnold Galombik remembered the bartering that took place for goods in his mother's shop on Rietkloof, and how, after a wheat season, they would have about 200 bags of wheat, weighing about 200 lb (90 kg) each and weighed on a little scale outside the shop. This threshing machine, the first in Namaqualand, shows an early move to mechanised farming.
McMillan collection, Manuscripts & Archives, UCT

they came to live in Springbok.

Joe brought administrative skills and legal knowledge to the new partnership with Jaap du Plessis as well as the motor car agency and Jaap provided the mechanical skills. They had not been in business long before they had to step in to help the town by starting a transport service. In June 1930, the South African Railways summarily terminated its uneconomic road motor service from Bitterfontein, the railhead 180 km south of Springbok, giving the public a mere 24 hours' notice of this action. It was a huge shock to the village which was left without a supply link between Bitterfontein and Springbok. Goods piled up at Bitterfontein station and the shopkeepers were in a panic about how to obtain supplies. Boris Saharin and David Gelb approached the partners, Joe and Jaap, for help and Jaap came up with a plan – '*nou hoekom bou ons nie 'n lorrietjie nie?*'[9] – to build a hybrid truck out of an old Buick motor car, which had been in an accident, and parts from a 1 1/2 ton Chevrolet truck. The makeshift truck was named Plaatjie and Joe and his wife, Bessie, themselves drove the truck to Bitterfontein and back to Springbok. In the early stages, the partnership had six lorries and the partners took turns at the driving. By 1934, with a contract for transporting materials to Vioolsdrift where a canal was being built to help the local farmers, their fleet had been increased to 20 3-ton Chevrolet lorries. New drivers were employed, both Coloured and white.

Jewish involvement in secular affairs, too, stepped up when Joe Jowell arrived on the scene. Joe was very interested in civic affairs and believed in the importance of local government. He had good mentors in Israel Gordon and Max Shapiro. In 1933, four years after he arrived, Joe, then aged 27, recommended that the village of Springbok become a municipality. There were financial advantages to this course, not the least of which was that it would provide access to bank loan facilities, which the village needed to provide much needed public amenities and services – beyond the scope of a Village Management Board. Elections were duly held and Israel Gordon, Joe Jowell, Max Shapiro, Jaap du Plessis, D J Basson and Jan Kotze were elected to the Municipal Council. Israel Gordon became the first mayor and three years later, Joe Jowell, then aged 30, succeeded him. He would remain mayor of the town for most of the following 27 years – his was an energetic, hard-working and active participation in local affairs.

The new Municipal Council inherited the endemic problems of water, sanitation and the commonage. There was, however, progress on all fronts. Piet van Heerde, principal of the school in Springbok, writes that it was because of the tact and determination of Joe Jowell that problems with the O'okiep Copper Company were resolved. A hospital was built in 1933 and in 1936 Springbok acquired electricity.

The small secondary school improved under the leadership of Piet van Heerde. 'Oom Piet', as he was known, had arrived in 1926 and with him arrived modern education. He was the brother-in-law of Reverend A G Driessen, then minister of the Dutch Reformed congregation of Namaqualand. The small secondary school soon became a high school. Most of the Jewish children

Deputation to Minister of Mines

The deputation from Namaqualand who met the Minister of Mines, Mr J H Hofmeyr, in February 1937 in connection with the re-opening of the copper mines. The members included farmers ('Oom' Bertus Roux, bottom right), professionals (Israel Gordon, lawyer, front middle and his partner Jan Scholtz, top, third from right), businessmen (Joe Jowell, middle row, centre), politicians (Daantjie Scholtz, MPC, also a lawyer, middle row, second from right and Jan Studer, ex MP, top, second from right).
Cape Times, Feb. 1937

started off school in Springbok and many tell of their experiences. Ellis Caplan remembered his first day at school when he was asked his name. 'Ellis' he said. '*Maar Alice is 'n meisie se naam*'[10] the teacher replied and from then on, to the annoyance of his mother, he was called 'Harris'. He was '*klapped*'[11] over the head when he reported back on his homework that 'quay' was actually pronounced 'key' and not 'kway', and told '*in hierdie klaskamer is dit "kway"* !'[12]

The Great Depression of 1931-32 and the drought of 1932-33 seriously affected the farming community. The prices of staple products dropped drastically after the 1929 Wall Street crash – wool from 14d a pound in 1929 to 4d in 1932 and maize from 15s 4d a bag of mealies to 9s 4d over the same period. The drought in the early thirties was one of the longest and severest experienced so far that century – it has been described as an '*allesvernietigende droogte*'.[13] The promised reopening of the copper mines had not taken place, and mining operations at Concordia and O'okiep had ceased in June 1931. Prosperity resulting from the discovery of diamonds had been short-lived. After the collapse of the diamond market in 1931, the diamond diggings at Kleinsee closed down the following year and many local workers were laid off. There was therefore no alternative employment on the mines for struggling farmers. In addition, many Namaqualand farms were too small to be economically viable. This was a result of a century-old tradition whereby each son inherited a portion of his father's farm.[14] Many a Namaqualand farmer was thus forced to seek work in the cities and joined the growing ranks of 'poor whites'. The Carnegie Commission into the Poor White Problem wrote in 1931 of the great need for able leaders to work with the farming communities in the country districts.

In Namaqualand, it was Albertus Myburgh Johannes Roux, known as 'Oom Bertus' who took the lead in helping the Afrikaner farmers win back their self-respect and self-confidence. Oom Bertus came from a lineage that loved the land and was involved in the community. He recognised that co-operative marketing was needed to save the stockfarmers in Namaqualand and became energetically involved in starting farmers' co-operatives throughout the region. He became chairman of the

Solomon Kluk, Garies

Businessman and developer in the town, Solomon Kluk described himself in the 1950's in a letter to *Die Burger* newspaper thus: 'I am a Jew who has spent a great deal of my life on the platteland and who has identified himself with the Afrikaner's way of life and ideals ...the Afrikaner is perhaps one of the few Christian nations that has treated the Jewish immigrant in a Christian manner and has never exercised social ostracism against him ... The Jew and the Afrikaner are perhaps the only two small nations in the world who are so desirous of guarding their group identity in very difficult circumstances.'
Harold Berman collection

Solomon's Kluk's store in Garies

Solomon Kluk's general dealer's store in the main street of Garies circa 1944.
Harold Berman collection

Boere-Unie van Namakwaland in 1935, remaining in that position until 1960, and chairman of the Namakwaland Vleiskoop Bpk from 1936-1962. The economic movement to establish a base for Afrikaner capital accumulation in the industrial and commercial sectors of the economy had begun.[15]

The establishment of farmers' co-operatives would have a severe impact on the Jewish traders, as we shall see later. But more ominous than these co-operatives was the emergence of political movements among the Afrikaners, more particularly right-wing groups who were radically anti-Semitic. The seeds had been sown years back. Men like Manie Maritz had a long history of obsessive Afrikaner nationalism and did not hesitate to use any opportunity to castigate the Jews. At a public gathering in Makwassie in the Northern Cape in 1924 he said: 'We have recently learned a great deal about the poverty of our people in the Northern Cape and Namaqualand. Who are responsible for this? Our arch-enemy the Jews who come to this country with a bundle on their backs and always manage to amass a large sum of money. The Afrikaners of those districts were virtually the servants of the Jews. It is similar in other parts of South Africa, and a people who made their money here out of the suffering of the people usually left the country and spent it somehow elsewhere.'[16] This public outburst attracted substantial press coverage and condemnation.

Maritz had delivered similar invectives to a gathering of diggers in Lichtenburg in 1926, identifying Jews as bloodsuckers and accusing them of dominating the Afrikaner. So the relationship between the farmers and the Jews who 'carried' them throughout the lean years, far from being viewed as genuinely helpful, became the basis for much animosity toward the Jew.[17]

Professor Milton Shain refers to the 'negative Jewish stereotype' that was developing in the country at that time, a view that was exacerbated by the collapse of the New York Stock Exchange in October 1929. There were calls to restrict immigration in the late 1920s and terms such as 'alien influences', 'racial stocks... unsuitable to the peculiar conditions of this country' and 'we want producers [not traders]' entered the immigration debate. In January 1930 The Immigration Quota Bill was introduced which 'limited to a numerical quota immigrants of whatever race or creed, born in quota or 'non-scheduled' countries. These were Greece, Latvia, Lithuania, Poland, Russia and Palestine (the only mandated country specifically named). Obviously, Jewish immigration from Eastern Europe was directly affected. The Quota Bill was assented to on 11 March 1930.[18]

In October 1933, the South African Christian National Socialist Movement – better known as the 'Greyshirts' – was formed under the leadership of Louis T Weichardt.[19] The Greyshirts were inspired by Hitler's success and tactics and followed fascist philosophies. There were cells throughout the country and by 1935 the South African Jewish Board of Deputies reported that anti-Jewish activities had reached an unparalleled height. In 1936 the Board of Deputies was in possession of information that Greyshirt candidates would be standing as Independents in Namaqualand in the forthcoming Provincial Council elections.[20] The 1939 election also saw the emergence of the Ossewa-Brandwag, (Oxwagon-sentinel) a paramilitary authoritarian movement and Nazi clone. 'Jew baiting' tactics were used to win support for the new Afrikaner Nationalist faith. Dr D F Malan, leader of the Cape National Party, indulged in such rhetoric during his 1938 political tour of Namaqualand in an attempt to convert the uneducated 'poor whites' and *bywoners* (share-croppers).[21]

Then, in 1939, the Second World War broke out. The Greyshirts and General Manie Maritz were active in Namaqualand and tried to incite the farmers to boycott the Jewish stores. Neither the Greyshirts nor Manie Maritz's anti-Jewish invective, it would appear, found an audience among Namaqualand Afrikaners. Solomon Kluk, a Garies storekeeper at the time, firmly believes this. He maintains that co-operation remained the practice in Namaqualand. Kluk had first-hand knowledge of this co-operation because he had been involved in much of the development in Garies since opening his store there. He dealt in building materials as well as in wool and skins, so was therefore able to undertake building projects in the town, such as the police station and post office. He got to know the Afrikaans farming community very well and built up an excellent relationship with them (supplying them with *kerkorrels*[22] as well). Such was his relationship with the Afrikaners that he became the only Jewish supporter in Namaqualand of the National Party, which came to power in 1948 under Dr D F Malan. He said that he liked the Afrikaners more than the Englishmen.

Kluk believed that incidents of destructive behaviour

Off to war

The Rabinowitz brothers, Sol, Joe and Hyme, who volunteered for the army during the Second World War, preparing at a training camp in Potchefstroom before going into the Abyssinian Campaign circa 1940. Note the gasmask kits around their necks.
Hyme Rabinowitz collection

SAWAS

The Saharin family moved from Springbok to Nababeep in 1938 and during the war years Milly Saharin involved herself with the local mining women and their war efforts such as the SAWAS (South African Women's Auxilary Service). Fund raising for the work of SAWAS through cookery and flower-arranging demonstrations would have suited Milly well – these were her particular skills. Here she is pictured left in the row directly behind the visiting commandants of the SAWAS and alongside the nurse-aides.
Saharin collection

which could be regarded as anti-Semitic, for example, when the petrol pumps at his store in Pofadder were torn down, were a result of youthful delinquency and alcohol rather than anti-Semitism. Cecil Jowell, younger son of Joe and Bessie, who grew up during the war years in Namaqualand, later said 'I still believe that these random negative remarks about Jews were not true anti-semitism ... but merely gratuitous comments used almost for lack of other epithets not directed at (or with the knowledge of) the Jews as a people and not really with any malicious or meaningfully critical intent'.

This view would seem to be substantiated by the South African Jewish Board of Deputies who reported in 1940 that 'the relationship between Jews and Gentiles is of the friendliest and that there are no untoward instances to report'.[23] A case in point would seem to be the relationship between Lulu Rabie and her Jewish friends. Lulu Rabie promised Bessie Jowell during the war that if the Nazis came to South Africa – and indeed, Robey Leibbrandt, the Nazi, did in fact land by submarine on the west coast – she would take care of Bessie's sons and raise them as her own.

During the war, many young Jews joined up so that for most of the war years there were not enough men to make a *minyan* on Friday nights in Springbok – the Gelb boys, Rabinowitzs, Caplans, Schaperas and Sidney Windisch all enlisted. We do not have the figures for the enlistment of the general Namaqualand population. A report in *Die Suiderstem* on 12 May 1941 quoted

Boris and Milly Saharin

Boris and Milly Saharin photographed behind his shop in Nababeep during the war years. The couple continued to be active in communal activities for all the years they lived in Namaqualand. *Saharin collection*

Chief Rabbi Israel Abrahams and Mrs Abrahams

Chief Rabbi Israel Abrahams and his wife on a communal visit to Namaqualand in July 1940. Picture taken outside the synagogue. *David Levy collection*

Mr J A Smith, assistant commandant-general of the Ossewa-Brandwag, as saying to an audience in Kamieskroon that the Ossewa-Brandwag fought against 'Jewish Imperialism and Capitalism and despised those who enlisted in the army for money'.[24]

During these war years, the Chief Rabbi of the Cape, Rabbi Israel Abrahams and his wife undertook a pastoral tour of the Northern Cape visiting Upington, Vanrhynsdorp, Springbok and Calvinia. They visited the Namaqualand community in July 1940. It was a busy week-end schedule for the Rabbi which included a Friday night service in the shul, supper at Rev G Gad's and a meeting with non-Jewish dignitaries including the Predikant of the Dutch Reformed Church at the Jowell home afterwards; on Saturday morning a children's service at the shul and a party for the children at the Jowell home, followed by a meeting with the Women's Zionist Society ladies; on Sunday a visit to the Nababeep copper mine in the afternoon and a meeting of the Congregation members, who came from all over the countryside, in the evening. The visit was an inspiring and uplifting one for the community.

Twins fishing for kreef

The Rabinowitz twins fishing for crayfish which they used as bait or threw back into the ocean. There had always been an abundance of crayfish in the Port Nolloth waters. As a consequence of that, the Ovenstones, who were very involved in the crayfish industry at the Cape, had built a canning factory among the dunes in 1919, run for many years by Andrew Ovenstone.
Hyme Rabinowitz collection

12 LIFE AT THE COAST

Port Nolloth was a unique Namaqualand town. It was originally called Robbe Bay because of the many seals that were found there in the early days, and which were an important source of income for the Namaquas before the advent of mining. It was chosen as a more suitable port than Hondeklip Bay from which to transport the copper ore from the inland mines. Robbe Bay was renamed Port Nolloth after Commander Matthew Nolloth who surveyed and chartered what was, at the time, a little-known bay. A railway line from the mines at O'okiep (the only privately-owned line in the country) was completed in 1873 and the ore trucks were pulled first by mule traction and, from 1876, by steam engine. The town had its ups and downs. Serving the copper mines was its main *raison d'être* but in 1918 John Ovenstone opened a crayfish ('rock lobster' was the official government name) factory there, 'a factory built on sand dunes'.[1] This was lucky for the town because the following year, with the drastic fall in the price of copper after the First World War, the copper mines closed down. Crayfish, therefore, became the only reason for Port Nolloth's existence.

In 1926 the discovery of alluvial diamonds helped in the town's recovery as the local storekeepers were able to supplement their custom from the farmers with business from the crayfish and diamond industries and associated employees. In 1927 the South African Railways extended the line to Bitterfontein, 60 km south of Garies. The copper mines re-opened and mine management found it more economical to truck ore to Bitterfontein, instead of using the railway line from the mines to Port Nolloth. By 1944 the line was no longer in use and was eventually torn up.

Port Nolloth, circa 1905

An early picture of the Front Street (today known as Kusweg) in Port Nolloth, circa 1905, showing the narrow-gauge railway line, which linked O'okiep with Port Nolloth, running across the foreground. The general dealers Smith and Webster, to the left, and William Carstens, to the right, appear in the middle ground. *H.R. Moffatt collection, National Library of South African, Cape Town*

But in 1939 the port was still busy and the town flourishing. The copper mines had reopened, diamonds were booming and the fishing boats were busy.[2] During the Second World War the Jews of Namaqualand holidayed in the cool seaside resorts of Port Nolloth and Hondeklip Bay where they could escape the intense summer heat of the interior. They were memorable holidays for both visitors and locals. Families travelled to Port Nolloth by steam train, because of petrol rationing, each family in their own coach, coupled together for the full day's journey. The journey was lots of fun for the children whose parents took food in hampers and toys to keep them occupied. Raphael Gelb remembers the train stopping and reversing to retrieve his sister's doll that she had thrown out of the window!

Aeroplane on the salt pan

With the advent of flying, the salt pan at Port Nolloth was used as a landing strip. This picture shows an aeroplane from Windhoek, then South West Africa, en route to Cape Town, which landed on the salt pan at Port Nolloth to collect passengers in the early 1930s. Cissy Rakoff travelled on that plane but is not pictured in the photograph.
Cissy Rakoff collection

The Cape Copper Company train

The Cape Copper Company train that ran from O'okiep to Port Nolloth from 1873 until the 1920s when it was 'vanquished' by the motor-lorry. Initially pulled by mules, steam engines had replaced mule traction by 1893. Today 'Clara' the mountain engine still stands in front of the museum in Nababeep – a great favourite with the schoolchildren. The railway line was torn up in 1944.
Betty Wright collection

On the Jetty

Arthur and Marlene Rosenberg on holiday from Garies standing on the jetty in Port Nolloth circa 1942.
Rosenberg family collection

Cricket on the salt pan

A combined team photograph of the first cricket match between Kleinsee and Port Nolloth on Blaau Pan, a salt pan at Kleinsee, 26 December 1931. The Port Nolloth team included Joe Rabinowitz (front, 2nd left), Joe Simon (front, 3rd left) and Sam Bolon (front, 5th left). Also in the picture is William Carstens (middle row, extreme left, in suit, tie and hat) and Jack Carstens (middle row, 4th from left). William Carstens, doyen of the old guard of the village (Port Nolloth) had a store on the front which was strategically placed for all the copper company employees leaving work when pay was still in golden sovereigns. Jack, his son, started the diamond rush in Port Nolloth in 1926 and by this stage was Mine Superintendent at Kleinsee and captain of the cricket club. He is seated wearing a colours cap in the middle row. Another interesting character is Jack Meadows (back row, extreme right, in white coat with hat). He ran the train from Port Nolloth to O'okiep as guard, conductor and everything else except driver and brakeman.

Joe Rabinowitz collection

At the crease

At the crease during the first cricket match between Port Nolloth and Kleinsee. Joe Rabinowitz bowling, Jack Carstens was the Kleinsee captain and Jack Meadows was the umpire. Matches were also played in Port Nolloth on the salt pan in the sand dunes outside the little town. This cricket pitch dated back to the end of the 1890s. It was such a grim walk to the salt pan that a special branch line was built from the seafront to the cricket pavilion and a special train was run to every match in the early days.

Joe Rabinowitz collection

Dancing on the pan

Dancing on the salt pan after the match. Batsmen Sam Bolon, who worked in the hotel and schoolboy Joe Rabinowitz, sporting his SACS school cap, pictured here.

Joe Rabinowitz collection

Rakoff se winkel

David Rakoff's shop or 'Rakoff se winkel' as it was called by the locals, sold groceries, dress materials, kitchen stoves, timber, traded in hides and sheepskins and was licensed to sell fireworks – truly a 'one stop shop'!
Cissie Rakoff collection

David and Bertha Rakoff

David, shopkeeper in Port Nolloth, and his wife Bertha, 1927
Cissie Rakoff collection

The town was mainly English with a lifestyle that was more suited to colonial India than South Africa – the inhabitants at the turn of the century were mostly Cornishmen, people from St. Helena and 'Hottentots'.[3] The bungalows or cottages on the seafront were old Cornish mining houses, wonderful little constructions, their floors, walls and ceilings made of imported Oregon pine or yellowwood and with corrugated iron roofs and wide verandahs. Historically they reflected the stratification of society in the early days of Port Nolloth's mining history. The front row of houses had been the homes of the magistrate, ministers of religion, doctor, owners of hotels and stores and company managers. Behind them, in the second row of smaller, lower houses, lived the carpenters and artisans, joiners and painters – all employees of the Cape Copper Company – while at the end of the village were the houses of the labourers. There was a clubhouse with a billiard room (with a picture of Lord Kitchener on the wall), a reading room with sports trophies, the latest English magazines and leather armchairs. There was a tennis club (tea and tennis biscuits were served) and a cricket club with Sunday games played on the saltpan. Golf was also played on the saltpan and later this same surface would be used as a landing strip for small aircraft.

Like the rest of Namaqualand, Port Nolloth was home to some thriving Jewish businesses and entrepreneurs. David Rakoff, for instance, was a shopkeeper who came by steamer to Port Nolloth in 1911. He married Bertha Woolf in 1923, whom he met while travelling to and from Cape Town on business. Bertha's father was a shopkeeper in Vanrhynsdorp. They had four children, three of whom (Julius, born in 1926, Vivian in 1928 and Riva in 1930) lived in Port Nolloth as small children.

Beach Road, Port Nolloth

Beach Road, Port Nolloth, showing the Commercial Hotel.
Cissie Rakoff collection

Roman Catholic Mission circa 1950

There were three churches in Port Nolloth: Anglican, Dutch Reformed and Roman Catholic. The Roman Catholic Mission, next to the lighthouse on the seafront, was a simple, corrugated iron building with a steeple and glass window through which one could see a plaster figure of the Virgin and Child – the only public display of 'art' in Port Nolloth, according to Vivian Rakoff. The Roman Catholic sisters of the Oblates of St Francis de Sales had been there since the early twentieth century when they had opened a school for Coloured girls where reading, writing, embroidery and music were taught. The nuns were educated women with a 'marvellous' Mother Superior, Sister Raphael who was Belgian. Bertha Rakoff and Sister Raphael became good friends and when Bertha's daughter, Riva, later married David Levick, she received for her wedding 'the most beautiful handmade lingerie and table cloths' made by the nuns.
Cissie Rakoff collection

The youngest, Eugene, never did but spent many holidays there.

David Rakoff's shop, or 'Rakoff se winkel' as it was called by the locals, sold groceries, dress materials, kitchen stoves and, unusually for a country dealer, timber. There was the usual trade in hides and sheepskins which still evoked vivid memories in his elder son, Vivian, years after: 'piles of hides made into neat bundles with rope, my father's initials "DRPN" stenciled on the uppermost skin in a vivid blue dye. Whatever happened to the hides later made them very different from the stiff, salt-caked, hairy, flat things that were tied up for shipment'. The notice board above the store read 'D. Rakoff, General Dealer' and carried a little addition 'Licensed to sell fireworks' – the local people commemorated Guy Fawkes.

Rakoff acted as wholesaler and retailer, which was also unusual for a country storekeeper. He supplied other stores, he had a contract with the diamond diggings to provide groceries for the workers at Alexander Bay and he supplied Ovenstones Canning Fisheries with goods. So, whereas other stores suffered when the copper mines were closed between 1919 and1937, Rakoff's business continued to operate.

David Rakoff also had a dairy and a bakery – the family had the only cow in the town. The milk from the cow was used for their household of children and the rest was given to the nuns of the Roman Catholic Church to use for sick children. He was the local philanthropist. Vivian Rakoff confirms that his father helped people with '*nagtmaal geld*' during the Depression and extended credit to those less fortunate than himself.

In addition to his shop, he also ran a hotel. The Marine Hotel, situated approximately 100 yards (90 m) from the Commercial Hotel, was a corrugated iron building built before the First World War by Joseph Dembitzer. In fact David Rakoff first came to Port Nolloth to assist Joseph Dembitzer in his hotel. Rakoff's hotel was a double-storied concrete and brick building with a big *stoep* on the front and a glassed-in balcony upstairs with big windows. It had a staircase with a wooden banister which the Rakoff children, Julius, Vivian, Riva and Eugene, delighted in sliding down. The hotel was one of the few masonry buildings in Port Nolloth.

Louis Rabinowitz was also a shopkeeper in Port Nolloth in the early years. He had started off as a *smous* operating from Porterville Road northwards and dealing mainly in horses and mules. He married a girl from Mossel Bay, Ellen Brodie, in 1914. Their first child, Joe, was born in Mossel Bay. Ellen and six-weeks-old Joe travelled to Port Nolloth in the small steamer '*Nautilus*', which carried some twenty passengers in addition to freight between Cape Town and Port Nolloth, and land-

The Rabinowitz family of Port Nolloth, 1925

The Rabinowitz's was a cultured home. It was filled with lots of books in German and High Dutch. Both Louis and Ellen were educated in Russia and spoke five languages between them – their home language was Yiddish. The children Joe, Bella, Freda, Sol, Hyme and Linkel had piano lessons, one of the Carstens girls taught piano, and music was provided by an old gramophone with a big horn. Louis Rabinowitz died in 1927 and was buried in the O'okiep Jewish Cemetery.
Hyme Rabinowitz collection

HYMIE RAKOFF
Fresh Fruit
& Vegetables.
Tobaccos.

ed them in a passenger basket – a scary experience. The Rabinowitzes were the only Jewish family in Port Nolloth – until David Rakoff married – and at Passover, Louis would don the frock coat and top hat in which he was married and Ellen would manage to get some flowers to adorn the table. Their Passover supplies would come in from M. Beinkenstadt in Cape Town.

There were many Jewish clerks working for the Jewish shopkeepers in the town, among them Joe Simon. He was one of five brothers who came from Leeds, England and who worked in Namaqualand. Joe came to Port Nolloth in 1929 and remained until 1942, working for David Rakoff. He was a keen cricketer and also became involved in civic affairs serving as chairman of the Village Management Board for a period. Brothers Jack and Dan were travelling salesmen, Harry worked in Springbok for nine years for David Gelb and Ike was in Port Nolloth briefly during the early years of the First World War. All were frequent visitors to the Rabinowitz household.

Several other Jewish shopkeepers, including Herman Klass and Hymie Rakoff came to Port Nolloth during the diamond rush. Hymie Rakoff, David's brother, ran a café and stayed for several years. In 1931 he married Cissie Koonin, whose father was a dentist and travelled throughout Namaqualand using a foot-driven drill. He made dentures from gold coins belonging to his patients, which he fashioned in his dental caravan. He was always accompanied by a fox terrier, which he had fitted with a gold filling. Hymie and Cissie stayed in Port Nolloth for two years.

During the war years Jewish life was organized around the few families that lived there – the Rabinowitzes, the Klasses, the Simons and the Rakoffs. Numbers were increased when the visitors from the interior came down during the summer holidays. Regular evening services could then be held, usually at the Rakoffs' home. Many of the visitors stayed at the hotels though some had their own homes – the Gordons and the Jowells, for instance. This was usually

◀ Clerks outside Hymie Rakoff's shop

Hymie Rakoff, a keen amateur photographer, took this photograph in 1929 of the clerks who worked in David Rakoff's store. Among them are Louis Solsky (on top), Joe Rabinowitz, still a school boy (second from bottom), Sam Stein, bookkeeper (bottom). Standing on the right, Mr Petaki. As businesses grew, there was a need for assistants and young, single Jewish men took the opportunity of working in the stores. Later some of them established their own businesses in the area and so the economy expanded. The products as advertised on the front walls of this shop – fresh fruit & vegetables, delicacies, confectioneries, tobaccos – would most likely have come by sea from Cape Town on the small sailing vessels that plied up and down the west coast.
Cissie Rakoff collection

Itinerant dentist

Zalman Koonin, the itinerant dentist, travelled around the countryside using a caravan. Made in Windhoek in 1926 by the builder of the Kaiser's coach, there was sleeping accommodation, a surgery and a mechanical room.
Cissie Rakoff collection

Hymie and Cissie Rakoff

Hymie Rakoff and his wife Cissie at the Cliffs, north of Port Nolloth, 1929, where diamonds had been found.
Cissie Rakoff collection

Cousins on holiday in Port Nolloth

Cousins Joyce Bernstein with Riva Rakoff, whose roots were in Namaqualand, on holiday in Port Nolloth in the 1950s. Children at boarding school in Cape Town also loved going home for the school holidays and often took friends with them.
Sarah (Chloe) Bernstein collection

over the Christmas and New Year period but also for weekends during the year. Families from Garies and other little *dorps* also came and in the evenings, families would walk along the beachfront before dinner – it was a 'ritual' said Riva Levick, one that is played out all over the world and which imbues a sense of holiday. The Coloured folk in their Christmas *rokke* (dresses) and Christmas *pakke* (suits) added to the festive atmosphere.

The mining crowd from O'okiep also came down during the summer, including Marcus Banghart, general manager of the O'okiep Copper Company at the time, and his wife Lurene and family. They made a special impression on the local families and introduced a 'sort of simple American Midwest touch into this Afrikaner/English/Jewish *mélange*, which was Port Nolloth' reminisced Vivian Rakoff. He remembered, too, the 'very American' children's parties – hot dogs, soft drinks, barbecues and toasting marshmallows on the beach. Riva Levick recalled the parties for young people at the Jowells, who were up to date with 'one of those wind-up record players' – she learned to dance in the Jowell house!

Cecil Jowell remembers those memorable holiday times in Port Nolloth, a familiar, eagerly anticipated, repeated ritual (every six weeks' holiday in December between 1939 – 1945): playing on the beach and under the jetty; going to the little island near the jetty in the dingy rowed by Michael Kling, the port's chief pilot; driving to McDougals Bay (and getting stuck regularly in the sand roads unless you had an expert driver like his father) and swimming and canoeing in the warm water; partying at the Gordons – Edward and Selina's house; trying to surf at Stilbay; the white roads contrasting with the usual Namaqualand brown; taking showers from a bucket hoisted to the ceiling; gas lights and meals with his father's friend, Captain Jonker, head of the South African Police for the Namaqualand area.

The Jowells retained their holiday homes (one of which is the original Aaron de Pass house) and later lent them to Grazia de Beer who used them as part of her guest lodge, Bedrock Inn. Ex Namaqualanders such as Hyme and Jeni Rabinowitz often stay there bringing family and friends.

Kids on roof

The Rabinowitz twins, Hyme and Sol, with their great friends, Jeck and Dougie Ovenstone.
Hyme Rabinowitz collection

Fun in the sun

Locals and holidaymakers on the beach at Port Nolloth. Among them L to R : Leah Klass, Dinah Rabinowitz, Cissie Koonin and Millie Gelb. Circa 1931.
Cissie Rakoff collection

Sights and sounds of Port Nolloth

Vivian Rakoff, reminiscing years later, recalled the sights and sounds of Port Nolloth in his childhood: 'Going to sleep was accompanied by a whole series of huge rhythms – the rhythm of the bell-buoy, the rhythm of the waves on the beach, the rhythm of the lighthouse and they became a cocoon of protection to me as a child growing up in Port Nolloth'.
Hyme Rabinowitz collection

A painter's view of the Kamiesberge

Oil painting of a scene near Springbok/Concordia showing the Kamiesberg in the distance. Artist Lady Esther Ellerman was a regular visitor to Namaqualand with her husband, Sir John Ellerman of the Ellerman and Bucknell Shipping Lines. Sir John was a keen naturalist and liked to escape the British winters by spending time in South Africa in the 1950s and 1960s.

13 DECLINING YEARS

In 1945, the Second World War ended. At around the same time, many Jews began to leave Namaqualand and head for the cities.

There are many reasons why Jews started leaving the country communities throughout South Africa after the Second World War – in fact the height of Jewish presence in the country districts according to census statistics was in 1936 so the decline probably started during the war. One of the reasons was the need for Hebrew education. Jewish boys were sent off for their Hebrew education, particularly in preparation for their *barmitzvahs*. Before 1945, they would attend secular school as well as the Talmud Torah or private Hebrew classes for their Hebrew education. A Jewish Day School in Cape Town, Herzlia, which also taught secular subjects, was started in 1945 and parents were encouraged to send their children to the school. Cecil Jowell comments on the consequences of sending children away from home at a young age as follows:

> The "trek" of Jewish boys aged 11 and 12 to the city from the country, in order to study for their *barmitzvahs* must have had a profound psychological effect on the parents and the children. While sending the youth off to boarding school may have been a particularly British trait, it was not that common elsewhere except for children far from any school such as farmers. But for the Jewish children coming from a close family life to be spirited away at a fairly young age, must have had a profound influence on their characters and independence. I had a generally very happy life at boarding school and university but am not sure that this was a universal experience or that in fact I did not lose some valuable growth influence.

Off to schul

Bertha Jowell and her two sons, David and Paul, dressed up and on their way to shul, early 1960s.

Young girls, too, were sent at an early age to Cape Town for their education. The trend escalated because, as the numbers started declining in the country, so communities stopped being able to afford Rabbis or Reverends.

Then there was the question of anti-Semitism. In some communities, anti-Semitism during the war was a precipitating factor. This was not the case in Namaqualand, as we have seen in a previous chapter, so it would not have been a primary reason. Young people who left the country for schooling, both Hebrew and secular, rarely returned. Certainly there was no reason to, if, as a result of the growth of the farmers' co-opera-

Joe Jowell

This photograph was taken at the prime of Joe Jowell's life and at the height of his involvement in Namaqualand – it epitomises the man and his world.

Three Jowell boys ▶

David, Michael and Paul, sons of Neil and Bertha Jowell, among the daisies on the Jowell farm during one spectacular Namaqualand flower season in the early 60s.

Sharon and Mark Jowell ▶

Sharon and Mark, children of Cecil and Phyllis, on the banks of the Orange River waiting for the flood waters to reach Vioolsdrift after heavy rains in the Transvaal had swollen the river. This was before the Hendrik Verwoerd (now Gariep) Dam was built which contained the floodwaters. Circa 1966.

tives, prospects were dim for expansion of the stores their fathers had established. During the 1930s farmers' co-operatives had become entrenched. In 1933 the first control boards were established by the Government to regulate the sale of produce. Wheat and maize sales were the first to be controlled, rapidly followed by many other products including beans and bananas! Farmers had to sell their agricultural produce directly to the control boards or their agents, the co-operatives. This meant that individual storekeepers and brokers could no longer buy directly from or trade with the farmers. There was now no longer a free market economy and many storekeepers were put out of business. Policies designed to save the farmers from economic ruin had the opposite effect on the small Jewish country storekeepers.

Also, a few Afrikaner-Namaqualanders had opened stores and in Garies, Kamieskroon and Springbok shops named Boere-winkel, Nasionale Winkel, Kontant-winkel, Geel-winkel and Ko-operasie-winkel appeared on the local scene.[1]

The Greyshirts in particular had tried to pressurize the farmers to boycott the Jewish stores, but many of the older Afrikaners continued to support the Jewish storekeepers regardless. However, business continued to decline and one by one the Jewish shopkeepers started selling up and joining their children in the cities. Some men continued to commute to Namaqualand to maintain their business interests but the family-base had now moved to the cities.

One exception to this trend in Namaqualand was the Jowell business. The hybrid truck named 'Plaatjie', which Jaap du Plessis had built when the South African Railways Road Motor Service to Namaqualand was withdrawn in June 1930, was to be the forerunner of a transport empire. An empire which, 60 years later, by the end of the 1980s, spanned the entire country.

Joe's sons, Neil and Cecil, were more fortunate than most in having a viable business to enter when they returned to Springbok after completing their tertiary education in Cape Town in the latter part of the 1950s. By then the business had grown considerably. The copper mines had reopened in 1937 and Jowells Transport handled the OCC's general goods transport and later all the excess coal from Bitterfontein station. The diamond mines on the coast, too, after they re-opened in 1943, required transport to the port at Port Nolloth and the mines at Oranjemund and the contract for all its road transport work was awarded by Consolidated Mines Limited to Jowells Transport in 1946. Jaap du Plessis had retired; Joe's brother, Simon, who had joined the business, had died and Joe was keen that his sons join him, especially after the company went public in 1955. At that time, Joe had travelled throughout Namaqualand selling shares in his company to the locals, hoping the new company, the Jowell Transport and Motor Company, subsequently Trencor, would benefit the Namaqualanders and that they would be the main shareholders. The company became the highest tax payer in Namaqualand with branches in Bitterfontein, Garies, Pofadder, Aggenys, O'okiep, Nababeep, Port Nolloth and Oranjemund, employing 1000 persons (equaling 10 000 dependants) and housing many of them.

Neil and Cecil thus returned to Namaqualand in the late fifties. Both were married to Cape Town girls. Neil's

Truck transporting sheep

A Jowells double-decker Leyland Comet truck transporting sheep in the late 1950s.

wife, Bertha, was a trained nursery school teacher and she started the first nursery school in Springbok – in her mother-in-law Bessie Jowell's back yard with an old aeroplane packing case serving as a wendy house. A new generation of Jowells started arriving – three sons were born to Neil and Bertha, and a daughter and son to Cecil and his wife, Phyllis. Both Bertha and Phyllis had their babies at home with the local doctor, Dr Neels Basson, in attendance, assisted by a local midwife.

Joe Jowell was still mayor of Springbok at this time and his daughters-in-law assisted Bessie with all the entertainment incumbent on an active mayor's spouse. Bessie regularly organized annual Children's Day celebrations for both Coloured and white communities – and always arranged entertainment such as puppet theatre for the children. She was a naturally hospitable and generous person, good at organizing, socially aware and comfortable across the social divide. The parties and functions she hosted, whether for Joe's business or his community obligations, saw an interesting mixture of guests from the village, the farming and the mining communities. She was as at home with the Archbishop of Cape Town as she was with the truck drivers' wives and was accessible to all. She spoke both English and Afrikaans fluently. She was a great asset to Joe and developed the woman's role to a high art. Bertha and Phyllis, encouraged by Bessie, also became involved in the various cultural, educational and charitable institutions in Namaqualand.

Joe had become Mayor of Springbok in 1937 and, except for one brief period, served in this role for more than 30 years. His success at the municipal polls was marked with a Mayoral Sunday for the community – in 1952 Rabbi Shrok of Cape Town officiated; in 1957 Chief Rabbi Israel Abrahams and in 1961 Rev Jossie Klitzner, also of Cape Town, officiated. Joe served on the local municipal and divisional councils, sports bodies such as the rugby board, charitable institutions such as SANTA and the Red Cross and, by branching out into the regional, national and international areas of these bodies, succeeded in putting Namaqualand on the international map. Also, in his capacity as president of the SA Road Federation for many years (1962 - 1972) and as senior vice-president of the international body, and as president of the SA Motor Trade Association (1958 - 1972) and a vice-president of the international body (the first South African ever to be elected), he promoted Namaqualand and South Africa. By the end of the 1960s, he was being hailed as the 'Uncrowned King of Namaqualand'. Joe's success was due to his hard work and total dedication to his business and to Namaqualand and its peoples. Theunis Uys writes:

> *Hy het meer tot die infrastruktuur van Namakwaland bygedra as die lot verantwoordelike politici wat Namakwaland verteenwoordig het, tesame. Hy het 'n groot invloed gehad by die teer van Namakwalandse paaie, watervoorsiening aan Springbok en ongewing, opgradering van afdelingspaaie, gesondheidsdienste (veral tuberkulose), telefoondiens, posdiens en die daarstelling van 'n plaaslike lugdiens.* [2]

One of Joe Jowell's great successes, and where he left his mark as an outstanding arbitrator, was the resolution of the longstanding, controversial trekpath issue amongst the Namaqualand farming community. Historically, the pioneer farmer in Namaqualand had been a nomad, following his flocks through open land. Times had changed. The great plains had been divided into farms and given to the farmers on reasonable conditions. The farmers mostly owned both a winter grazing farm in the Sandveld and a summer grazing farm in Bushmanland. Then, mainly because of the jackal problem, they began fencing off their farms with jackal-proof fencing. This meant that less and less free ground became available for the *trekboers* who were still nomadic and the farmers who trekked between their winter and summer grazing properties. This led to

Frikkie Oppel, the first driver

Frikkie Oppel, the first driver for the Jowells transport company, remained with the company for many years. Here he is pictured in the cabin of his truck in 1958.

Hy het meer ... : 'He did more for the infrastructure of Namaqualand than all the politicians put together. He had a huge influence on the tarring of the roads, the provision of water for Springbok and its environs, the upgrading of the region's roads, health services (in particular tuberculosis), the postal services and he initiated a local air service'.

Jack Sovinsky at his rutile mine

Note the primitive conditions with which adventurous prospectors had to contend.
Sovinsky collection

much dissent among the farmers and many Commissions of Enquiry were held on the trekpath issue. It was only during Joe Jowell's era at the Divisional Council that, with his tact and diplomacy, the problems were finally sorted out and the matter resolved in 1959 with a unanimous decision that trekpaths cease to be officially proclaimed. All this despite his poor eyesight and heart block (which he developed in 1948 and for which the doctors gave him a life expectancy of six months).

There were other successful, interesting Jewish characters who contributed to life in Namaqualand during those declining years of Jewish presence. Jack Sovinsky, for instance, who had arrived in Namaqualand many years earlier, had married and settled down with teacher Sybil Sacks. Their two daughters, Doreen and Isobel, grew up in Springbok. Jack acted as the Cantor in the synagogue for many years but he had another claim to fame – he was known as the '*klipdoktor*' of Namaqualand because of his knowledge and expertise in mineral exploration. At the Sovinsky's 25th wedding anniversary in 1952, the local MP for Namaqualand, Daantjie Scholtz, said of Jack that he had 'opened up the mineral wealth of Namaqualand'. His wife, Sybil, told how he had got caught up, as a young man, in the excitement of the diamond rush and with that acquired a taste for prospecting which 'set a pattern for him for the rest of his life'. He prospected for all sorts of base minerals – beryllium, tungsten, columbite and tantalite, amongst others. Dealing in base minerals was his main business – a 1955 photograph of the shop, 'J Sovinsky (Edms) Bpk', advertises him trading in hides, skins, peas and beans and second-hand furniture as well. The Sovinskys left Springbok in 1961. Jack had been there since 1917.

Other stalwarts of the Jewish community were the Gelbs, Neumanns, Shulmans, Jacobs, Silvers, Ginsbergs, Abramsons, Levys, Udwins and Windisches. All raised families there. Brothers Oscar and Conrad Shulman ran the pharmacy and a gents' outfitter in Springbok; Harold and Raphael Gelb started a wholesale business there; the Levys, Abramsons, Jacobs, Silvers and Windisches had stores; Walter Neumann and Nathan Ginsberg worked on the mines and the Udwins ran the Springbok Hotel (Joyce Udwin was the daughter of the Tepersons who had bought the Garies Hotel from the Rosenbergs before moving over to the Springbok Hotel). The Smeimans were seasoned hoteliers in Namaqualand – during its golden years Max ran the Springbok Hotel, and his sons Julius and Bennie ran the Port Nolloth and O'okiep Hotels just after the Second World War.

Walter Neumann joined the O'okiep Copper Company in 1945 as Electrical Engineer. He had an interesting and successful career with the Company and was promoted a number of times – by 1964 he occupied the senior position of Resident Engineer. He was

Jack Sovinsky

Jack Sovinsky in front of a matjieshouse where he was negotiating for the purchase of wool; and (above) standing in front of his storehouse with bags of wool.
Sovinsky collection

The Shulman brothers

Connie Shulman (on the left) ran a men's outfitters and Oscar, his brother, was the local pharmacist. They came to Springbok in 1952, married and raised families there and stayed almost twenty years.
Shulman family collection

Father and sons

Aubry, Mark and Harry Abramson. Harry was still running his jewellery store in Springbok in the 60s when the boys came home on holiday from Cape Town.
Aubry Abramson collection

instrumental in restoring the historic Cornish pump engine, built and installed in 1882 when the O'okiep mine was at the height of its production, and ore containing 15 000 tons of copper was exported each year. The engine remained in operation until 1929 and was restored and reassembled under his supervision in 1965.

Walter, together with Harry Abramson, conducted Friday night services in the synagogue in the 1960s, when the community was seriously in decline, and assisted at High Festivals.

Rosalyn, Walter's wife, whom he married in 1954, kept a *kosher* home for her family. Her parents, the Shannons, sent *kosher* meat from Cape Town by train to Bitterfontein station where it was collected and transported by the Jowells Refrigerator Service. One *Yomtov* the Shannons flew by Jowell plane from Cape Town, bringing with them bottles of mead (a sweet beer drunk during Passover). The passengers were concerned when they heard something popping at a certain altitude and only when they noticed a trickle of liquid running down the aisle of the little twin-engine aircraft, did they realize what had happened – the bottles of mead were exploding, one by one! It was difficult being a traditional Jewess in a mining environment, where one entertained, and was entertained a great deal. Rabbi Duchinsky, in one of his pastoral reports, credited her with persistence and resilience in maintaining her *kashrut* standards there.

Both Walter and Rosalyn were involved with charitable work in Namaqualand, Walter with SANTA in its fight against tuberculosis, rife in Namaqualand, and Rosalyn with the Red Cross Society, the local branch of which was started in 1941 by Milly Saharin and Lurene Banghart, wife of the mine manager.[3] The Red Cross, amongst its other tasks, was often called upon to organize relief operations for the victims of the floods that occurred when the Orange River came down in flood and burst its banks. This was before the Hendrik Verwoerd Dam, now known as the Gariep Dam, was opened in March 1972.

Life in the 1950s was peaceful and tranquil for the Jews of Namaqualand, as it was in the rural areas generally. Families felt safe, they slept with doors and windows open. Children could walk to school or take their bicycles to the village. Life was simple in the country. Many children went to school barefoot – *dubbeltjies* (thorns) were the bane of Cecil Jowell's life. When the children grew up and left for schooling in the cities, they travelled together on the train from Bitterfontein station, stacked up with provisions prepared by their mothers. They mainly went to boarding school in Cape Town, the boys to SACS or Wynberg Boys' High and the girls to Good Hope Seminary High or Wynberg Girls' High. They loved coming home for the school holidays, often bringing friends from the cities.

Cecil Jowell reminiscences about growing up in Springbok and his comments reflect what many others feel about their own lives at that time:

> We grew up speaking English at home to our parents, and Afrikaans to everyone else … my brother and I were really not seen as different to everyone else by our peers – and particularly when we went elsewhere our language and looks (we were both fair and blue-eyed) made for people seeing us as *ware Afrikaners* [4]…
>
> But of course there were some differences. During assembly time on Mondays and Fridays, when it came for time for prayers, my brother and I alone left the hall (of 300 children) and (at my mother's insistence) stood outside till prayers were over … Of course, on *Rosh Hashanah* and *Yom Kippur* we stayed out of school. Our peers seemed to see these as minor idiosyncracies with no real significance ... We did, of course, know that we were different, but I don't think we felt it as being much more than that we could speak English fluently.
>
> There was no question that on Friday nights we went to shul, on *Yom Kippur* we fasted (half-days while we were small) and during *Pesach* we ate no bread or sweets. For two very short periods there was a Reverend who gave us *cheder* classes, and then of course after we had (for one year) studied in Cape Town (and had to go to boarding school in order to do so) we returned home to have our *barmitzvahs* – unusual in many ways but particularly because in Springbok there was only one *barmitzvah* every two years or more.

Walter Neumann and colleague on the site of the O'okiep Copper Company

Walter Neumann, Resident Engineer of the O'okiep Copper Company (on the left) and colleague on the site of the Nababeep mine, circa 1955.
Sovinsky collection

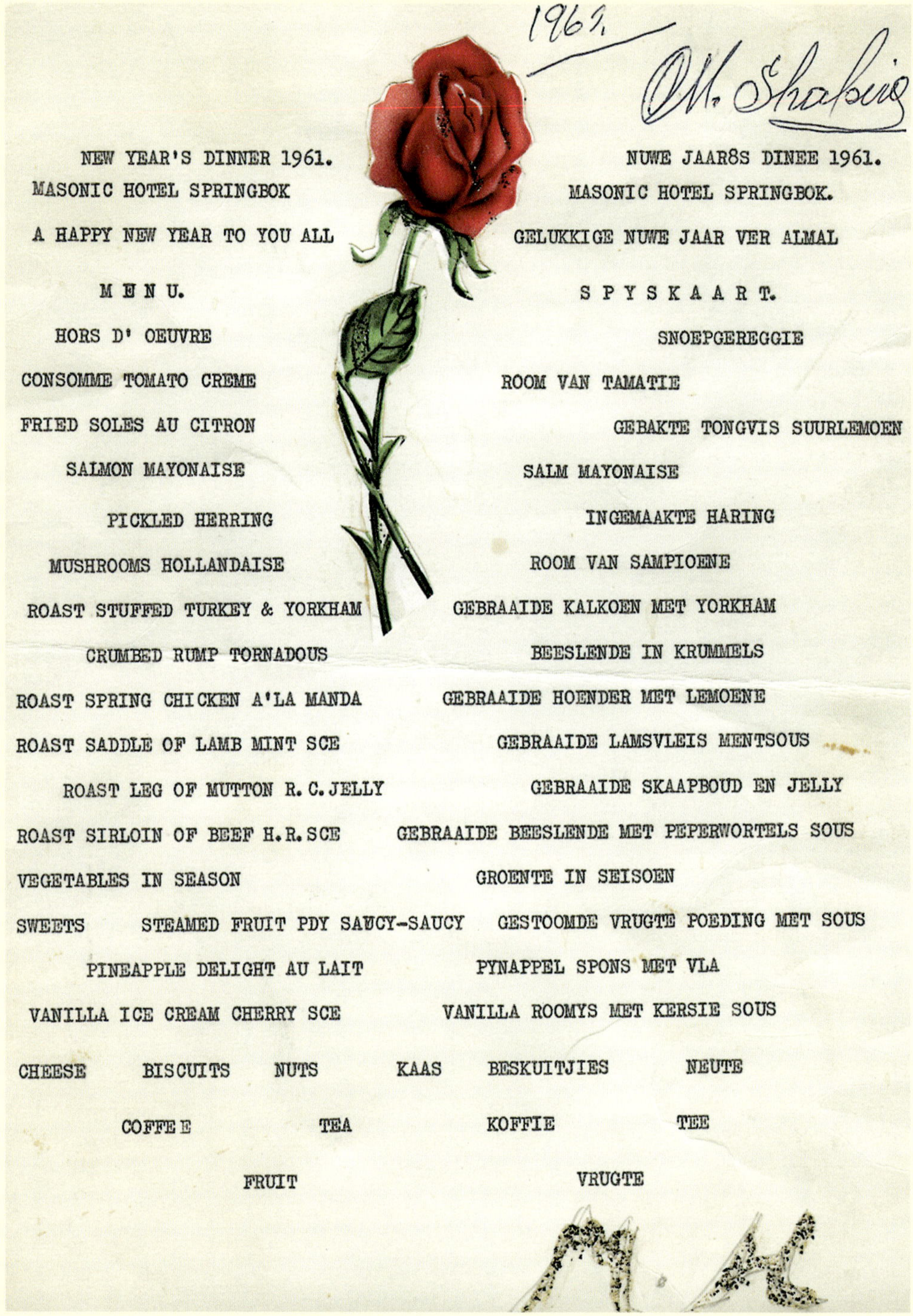

NEW YEAR'S DINNER 1961.	NUWE JAAR8S DINEE 1961.
MASONIC HOTEL SPRINGBOK	MASONIC HOTEL SPRINGBOK.
A HAPPY NEW YEAR TO YOU ALL	GELUKKIGE NUWE JAAR VER ALMAL
M E N U.	S P Y S K A A R T.
HORS D' OEUVRE	SNOEPGEREGGIE
CONSOMME TOMATO CREME	ROOM VAN TAMATIE
FRIED SOLES AU CITRON	GEBAKTE TONGVIS SUURLEMOEN
SALMON MAYONAISE	SALM MAYONAISE
PICKLED HERRING	INGEMAAKTE HARING
MUSHROOMS HOLLANDAISE	ROOM VAN SAMPIOENE
ROAST STUFFED TURKEY & YORKHAM	GEBRAAIDE KALKOEN MET YORKHAM
CRUMBED RUMP TORNADOUS	BEESLENDE IN KRUMMELS
ROAST SPRING CHICKEN A'LA MANDA	GEBRAAIDE HOENDER MET LEMOENE
ROAST SADDLE OF LAMB MINT SCE	GEBRAAIDE LAMSVLEIS MENTSOUS
ROAST LEG OF MUTTON R. C. JELLY	GEBRAAIDE SKAAPBOUD EN JELLY
ROAST SIRLOIN OF BEEF H.R.SCE	GEBRAAIDE BEESLENDE MET PEPERWORTELS SOUS
VEGETABLES IN SEASON	GROENTE IN SEISOEN
SWEETS STEAMED FRUIT PDY SAUCY-SAUCY	GESTOOMDE VRUGTE POEDING MET SOUS
PINEAPPLE DELIGHT AU LAIT	PYNAPPEL SPONS MET VLA
VANILLA ICE CREAM CHERRY SCE	VANILLA ROOMYS MET KERSIE SOUS
CHEESE BISCUITS NUTS	KAAS BESKUITJIES NEUTE
COFFEE TEA	KOFFIE TEE
FRUIT	VRUGTE

New Year's Eve Dinner 1961

The menu at the Masonic Hotel is still delectable!
Max Shapiro collection

'Shappy'

Max Shapiro, consummate hotelier and immaculate dresser, always affectionately known as 'Shappy'.
Max Shapiro collection

With the community in decline (there were only 23 Jews left in Springbok in 1961), a sense of having to survive permeated Jewish life – probably much like the start-up days. There was a strong sense of community and solidarity. Shappy initiated *le chaims* [5] after Friday night services at his hotel and this became a tradition. When he died in 1963, the tradition died with him. *Yomtov* time, communal meals and *seders* were celebrated together, either in the shul hall, the *succoth* alongside the shul, or in someone's home. The women would all make their specialities and bring them to the shul hall – Polly Abramson made the chopped herring, Bessie Jowell her famous potato salad, and Thelma Gelb her delicious chicken soup. Everyone looked forward to these speciality culinary contributions – except, of course, the husbands who had to transport the food in their cars. Woe betide if the pickled herring leaked on to the car seat – in the hot climate of Namaqualand, one would never get rid of the smell!

The SA Jewish Board of Deputies had started a programme of pastoral tours by Country Community Rabbis to service those communities who no longer had their own resident spiritual leaders (a trend throughout the country districts). In some declining communities, resident Rabbis combined communities and would minister to a number of them, but Namaqualand was too remote an area for this to be practical, so the new institution of pastoral tours was very helpful to the small Namaqualand community.[6]

The women's organizations continued to function. WIZO still boasted fifteen members in 1958 and continued with its fund-raising activities such as raffles and Zionist Balls. The balls remained a highlight of village life in Springbok, the only exception now being that musical entertainment, instead of being provided by the local bands, was provided by Cape Town bands such as the popular Vic Davis band. These were nerve-racking occasions for the organizing committee because the roads from Cape Town, still not tarred, often became impassable and the car carrying the band could get stuck in mud during wet weather or be stranded on the other side of the Olifants River when in flood! Still, Thelma Gelb, reminisced, 'we had our gramophones to fall back on'.

Amazingly, another women's group started up in the fifties. Sybil Sovinsky started the Union of Jewish Women in 1951 at the suggestion of Sarah Sloman, a key player in the national organization, who was on a visit to Namaqualand during the flower season. It was a chance remark, but that same evening they called a meeting at Sybil's house and started a local branch of the organization. Thelma and Beryl Gelb assisted Sybil in the offices of Secretary and Treasurer. So the same group of women raised funds for both these organizations – the Union of Jewish Women was geared to local charitable work and WIZO raised funds for Israel. Sybil later received the Sarah Sloman Award in 1986 for outstanding services to the organization. Certainly, the commitment and involvement of this handful of

Thelma Gelb

Thelma Gelb, Raphael's young wife, on holiday in Port Nolloth with friends circa 1946. Thelma and her sister-in-law, Beryl Gelb, between them handled the positions of Secretary and Treasurer respectively of the Jewish women's organizations for many years.
Selina Gordon collection

Springbok Hotel dining room

Masonic Lodge dinner at the Springbok Hotel after Cecil Jowell was installed as Master, September 1965. Phyllis Jowell on left, Joyce Udwin (proprietor together with her husband, Alec), on the right.

women was exemplary.

Although the size of the community was diminishing, the involvement and energy of those who remained was not. There were celebrations – the *barmitzvahs* of Arthur Rosenberg (in 1943), Neil and Cecil Jowell (in 1946 and 1948 respectively) and Mark Windisch (in 1946). The two hotels – the Masonic and the Springbok – provided venues for major functions. It was here that the Masonic Lodge dinners were held – in fact, between 1924 and 1965, 16 Jewish men had the honour of serving as master of the Lodge: Israel Gordon 1924; Julius Gordon 1927; Mick Caplan 1930; Ephraim Bernstine 1931; I M Hurwitz 1932; Joseph Jowell 1934 and 1935; Simon Jowell 1937; Jack Pachter 1938; Simon Jowell 1942; Joseph Jowell 1947; H R Gelb 1949; Raphael Gelb 1956; Neil Jowell 1962; Alec Udwin 1963; Monty Teperson 1964 and Cecil Jowell 1965. Chamber of Commerce and Lions of South Africa functions were also held in these hotels, which continued to be the focal point of country life. Joyce Udwin of the Springbok Hotel even started a nightclub on Saturday evenings, after the dining room was cleared, and there was dancing by candlelight – in keeping with the nightclub trend developing in the cities. Sunday lunches and New Year's Eve dinners were still a great draw-card.

Sybil Sovinsky

Sybil Sovinsky in her latter years. Photo taken by her granddaughter, Gillian Edelstein, showing her cheerful personality.
Sovinsky collection

Generally, there was a sense of togetherness and survival during these latter years of the Namaqualand Jewish community. Standards were maintained. Reinet Shulman, Oscar Shulman's wife, remembers going to shul on the *Yomtovim* 'in full regalia' – the women wore hats and when a visitor arrived who did not have a hat, she would be provided with one before she could attend the service in the synagogue.

Jonathan Shulman, eldest son of Oscar & Reinet Shulman, writing from Australia in 1994, where he now lives and practices as a radiologist, reminisces:

> Having been born in Springbok and lived there for nine years I still have fond memories of the town and surrounds... When I was growing up in Springbok, the Jewish community was very much on the decline. I can recall only a handful of families which were periodically complemented by Jewish travellers in town … I well remember a *Seder* at (the Jowell's) home in 1969 when being the only child present I had to ask the four questions. Having to read them in English was a task in itself since, other than at home, I spoke mainly Afrikaans. In fact I still have a *Haggadah* which Bessie inscribed and gave to me on the occasion. I have vivid memories of the shul and adjacent hall where many functions were held…

The relationship with the mining community (of which the management was largely American and Canadian), continued to be good. A solid business relationship existed between the Jowells and the O'okiep Copper Company; warm friendships were made and maintained on every level and there was co-operation on charitable committees, sports functions and social activities. Marcus D Banghart, who became general manager of the OCC in 1941 and who guided the company to great heights through his energy, enthusiasm, dedication and perseverance, like Joe, had faith in the potential of Namaqualand. He and Joe became firm friends. Banghart rendered liberal financial support for mineral exploration. He is regarded by many as contributing more to the revival and associated welfare of the people of the region at that time than any other individual. The mining industry left an indelible mark on Namaqualand in the fifty years after the mines reopened in 1937. The growth of towns like Springbok; the establishment of electrical power lines from the national power grid; the water pipeline from the Orange River supplying all the copper mines plus Steinkopf, Springbok and Kleinsee can all be attributed to the mining industry in Namaqualand at that time.[7]

The relationship with the wider community also continued to be good except for a period of anti-Semitism that started in the late fifties. In 1948 the United Party government had lost the general election to the National Party led by Dr D F Malan. The National Party's policy of racial discrimination or apartheid was implemented after their election victory and ultimately extended to virtually every sphere of life. In its early years apartheid was regarded as a means of consolidating Afrikaner nationalism and was used to ensure the economic empowerment of the Afrikaner.

In the 1950s a campaign was started by a group of Afrikaner Namaqualanders which blamed the transport monopoly and those who supported it, for keeping the railways out of Namaqualand and for the increasing hardships suffered by the farmers. This was despite the fact that when Joe Jowell's company went public in 1955, ordinary Namaqualanders were encouraged to buy shares in the company and thus could have been part of its success. On the whole, however, people mistrusted the offer and refused to buy shares. Having burned their fingers by investing in their own farmers' co-operatives might have influenced them as well. In 1959 Namaqualand was in the grip of yet another drought, which only exacerbated the situation and increased the levels of rhetoric.

This campaign gathered momentum in the early 1960s, and targeted the 'monopolistic capitalists', both Jewish and Afrikaner, who were also regarded as being

Spring festival

Drum majorettes in front of Springbok Hotel, spring festival early 1960s
Monty Teperson collection

politically too liberal. Men like Daantjie Scholtz, who had been the local Member of Parliament for many years, and Bertus Roux, chairman of the Farmers' Co-operative since 1935, were targeted as well as Joe Jowell. The campaign was spearheaded by a successful local farmer and included a medical doctor, some teachers, a businessman and the local DRC minister. It therefore differed from the anti-Semitism of the 1930s in that the individuals involved were professional people who were very concerned with the preservation of Afrikaner identity. Elections intensified anti-Semitic propaganda, with the slogan 'Don't vote for a Jew, vote for an Afrikaner' being bandied about. The sixties were thus a time of hurt, indignation and anger in a community that had been harmonious for so many years. Things eventually came to a head in November 1967, precipitated by Joe Jowell and Mayoral Sunday.

Joe had topped the polls in the current municipal elections and was again elected Mayor. He decided to celebrate his thirtieth year as Mayor with a Mayoral Sunday – a public service in the synagogue followed by a tea party arranged by the Jewish community in the local Church hall. The young *Dominee* of the Dutch Reformed Church (NGK) in Springbok, influenced by

Driver of the year

Neil Jowell, Martin Beukes and Cecil Jowell at the Jowells Transport Driver of the Year award in 1981. Martin Beukes personified the skills that the drivers brought to their work on the Namaqualand roads.

The Mayor who makes up a minyan

Joe first acquired a small plane in 1949. Although professional pilots worked for the company, both Neil and Cecil acquired pilot licenses and flew their father around. Here Cecil is in the cockpit with his father, June 1963.

the radical group, called on his congregation to boycott the occasion on religious grounds. This was despite the fact that on previous occasions there had been no issue with attending the service in the synagogue. But, such was Joe's standing in the community, the locals came in their droves and the function was well attended – much better than on previous occasions. The Namaqualanders also did not like being told what to do. Only the venue for the party after the service in the shul had to be changed – from the Church hall to the shul hall (the old synagogue). The public continued to support Joe overwhelmingly by voting for him at ensuing municipal elections. Years later, after Joe had died, the *Dominee* in question apologized to Bessie and explained that he had been very young, easily influenced and highly impressionable, and that he had been wrong.

How much of the antagonism directed at Joe Jowell and other successful and influential businessmen was due to anti-Semitism, radical Afrikaner nationalism or jealousy and envy is hard to assess. Certainly there were aspects of all of these, combined also with the belief prevalent among Namaqualanders at the time that 'life is about struggle'.[8] Individuals making a success in an environment which the locals thought even God had forgotten, were bound to be regarded with suspicion and envy. Politicians could easily manipulate these feelings to their own advantage.

Joe was ahead of his time in his thinking, attitudes, value system and fairness across the colour line. He believed in education and training and had always put his ideas into practice in his own businesses. In the early seventies, he was instrumental in establishing a training scheme for Coloured employees and, together with the O'okiep Copper Company and Kleinsee, sponsored a meeting of local industries in 1971 to discuss this scheme. He wrote letters to companies he thought would be interested in 'developing our Coloured workforce to its full potential'. To this end, he wrote to Ovenstones, Barlows, Consolidated Diamond Mines, Oranjemund, Pella, Unicorn Shipping and Coloured Affairs amongst others. At the meeting, he made an impassioned plea for the scheme to be accepted. The companies represented at the meeting, he said, had all taken a lot from Namaqualand and had made a good living there, and that this was an opportunity to put something back into Namaqualand. The scheme unfortunately was abandoned after discussions with the Commissioner for Coloured Affairs but the O'okiep Copper Company agreed to start something on a small scale at their training centre to train motor mechanics.

It would be over to Joe Jowell to keep the dwindling Jewish community together during the twilight years in

Joe and Bessie Jowell in their Chevrolet

Joe and Bessie Jowell still driving their 1955 Chevrolet in 1971.

Namaqualand. Already in the late fifties, it was becoming difficult to assemble ten men for a Friday evening service. 'Shappy' and Joe managed to keep the services going. Joe was called 'The Mayor Who Makes Up A Minyan'[9] – he would return home by airplane from his trips around the country in time for Friday night services, buzzing his secretary by flying low over the village. Joe's secretary, Anna Priem, played an invaluable role during these years, acting as unofficial *shammash* to the congregation, rounding up all the Jews and commercial travellers on Friday nights. She would not accept payment for the work she did for the congregation. Bessie and her helper, Ou Japie, kept the shul clean – Ou Japie swept the shul and its surrounds regularly. Bessie hosted many communal functions in her home.

Joe was President of the congregation from 1959 until its disbandment in 1972. His sons Neil and Cecil acted as treasurer and secretary respectively until Neil left Namaqualand in 1962 and Cecil in 1967. Joe had served as an office-bearer from 1929 until 1972 – 43 years. He died in Springbok in 1972 and was buried in the O'okiep cemetery.

Whereas at the beginning of World War II, there were 116 Jews in Namaqualand, by 1951 this number had declined to 65 and by 1961 to 23. By 1978 there were only two Jews left in Springbok, Rebecca Jowell and Kurt Nussbaum, the manager of Gelbs Wholesale. One hundred and twenty-five years had passed since the arrival of Aaron de Pass, the first Jew in Namaqualand. It had been a vibrant and remarkable history.

Kamiesberg landscape

Namaqualand daisy flowering season. Kamiesberg, September 2001.
Norman Morrison

DIEP SPORE

The early Jewish pioneers in Namaqualand were too busy making a living for themselves and their families to keep diaries or write their memoirs. Only Abe Schapera, the chronicler of Jewish life in Namaqualand, Solomon Rabinowitz and Tilly Gordon, who started writing a history of the Namaqualand Hebrew Congregation, recorded life in those early days. It has fallen to us to gather recollections and photographs from the remaining pioneers or their children who today live all over the world. Some descendants were conscientious collectors of documents and artefacts, such as Pauline Rothschild (born Saharin), but most had kept very little. Jopie Kotze, a third generation Afrikaans Namaqualander, also collected photographs and documents from Jewish ex-residents and their families who visited his café in Springbok during the Namaqualand wildflower seasons. Jopie also collected material during the two *Boere-Jode* reunions he organized in the decade of the 1990s, and has donated most of his material to us.

Secondary sources of information for this book included Jewish communal records such as Country Rabbis' reports, press cuttings and books on Jewish history from the South African Jewish Board of Deputies archives and library and the invaluable research being conducted into the South African Jewish country communities by the SA Friends of Beth Hatefutsoth in Johannesburg. Extensive secular sources came from material in the Cape Archives, University of Cape Town Libraries, Manuscripts and Archives Department, the National Library of South Africa (Cape Town branch) and a wide variety of general publications.

Our research has revealed that the majority of Namaqualand Jews came from Eastern Europe, mainly Lithuania. A few came from England. They started trickling in from the late 1880s and by the mid 1930s the population had reached its peak. After the Second World War numbers declined steadily until by 1978 only two Jews remained. The children were the first to leave – going to the cities for their Jewish and secular education. There they were exposed to other opportunities and rarely returned. The tradition of

Joanne Jowell

Joanne Jowell, on a family visit to the farm 'Tweedam' near Springbok in the spring of 1986.

The consecration of the tombstone of Rebecca Jowell

The consecration of the tombstone of Rebecca ('Bessie') Jowell, the last Jew to be buried in the Jewish cemetery in O'okiep, 1989. *Hymie Gordon collection*

entrepreneurship was broken. In any event, there was little prospect for growth in the small family businesses after the advent of the farmers' co-operatives. Eventually the parents sold up and followed their children. By the 1960s most Jews had left for the cities, mainly Cape Town, and by 1978 there were only two Jews living in Springbok.

Very few families stayed in Namaqualand for more than two generations, even during the earliest years. Today, the descendants of Namaqualand Jews are to be found all over the world, from Toronto to Sydney. Some left South Africa for political reasons during the apartheid years, others to further their careers through post-tertiary education. There are doctors, psychiatrists, lawyers, business people, information technologists, anthropologists, social workers and a diplomat.

The early Jews helped transform the Namaqualand economy from an agrarian system based on barter to a modern cash economy. Later Jews such as Israel Gordon and Joe Jowell, who were involved in social leadership and civic affairs, helped transform the villages into modern municipalities and, through their involvement in the Divisional Council, were instrumental in creating the infrastructure that exists in Namaqualand today.

Most Namaqualand Jews contributed in one way or another to the general welfare of the Namaqualand community. Donating to the building fund of the Dutch Reformed Church for their new stone church in Springbok in the early 1920s is a prime example; flood relief another; charitable work for organizations such as SANTA and the Red Cross Society, yet another. After they left, some created trusts – the Namaqualand aged homes and a clinic for pre-natal care are still beneficiaries.

Today, the only signs of Jewish presence left in Namaqualand are the cemetery in O'okiep and the synagogue in Springbok, now a museum. Supermarket chains, as well as many shops, confirm that the trading culture fostered by the Jewish entrepreneurs still exists. So does the transport business, although less substantial than it was in Joe Jowell's time. Tourism, because of the unique floral displays in springtime, proximity to the Orange River and adventure holidays and the uniqueness of the Richtersveld landscape, has become a major industry and the hospitality business is flourishing.

If the Jews left *'diep spore'* in Namaqualand, as Colla Swart and others believe, so did that remote and arid place leave its indelible mark on them. They return to Namaqualand to be uplifted and inspired by memories and to get in touch with their forebears and roots. They take their children and grandchildren so that they, too, will get a feeling for the simplicity and genuineness of those days and in the hope that Jewish country values will live on through them.

Diep Spore

A *middelmannetjie* on the way to Skilpad. The Skilpad Wildflower Reserve near Kamieskroon was acquired in 1988 by WWF South Africa (World Wide Fund for Nature) and consisted predominantly of shrubland and abandoned wheatlands. These old wheatfields today offer a spectacular display of Namaqualand daisies. The Reserve has been incorporated in the Namaqua National Park which aims to conserve its unique succulent and floral diversity and is run by South African National Parks. There is ongoing cultural mapping (early stone-age artefacts have been found); a tourism training project for sixteen local communities has been initiated and black rhino are being re-introduced.

NOTES

A Coincidence

1 edited by Phillida Brooke Simons, Johannesburg, 1986, p.97.

1 The pioneers arrive

1 Uys, Theunis, 'Die Jode van Namakwaland, Hulle Invloed op Kulturele, Maatskaplike en Ekonomiese Gebied', unpublished manuscript, 2003.
2 Johnson, Paul A., *A History of the Jews*, New York, 1987, p.359.
3 Norwich, Rose, 'Recording Our Past', *Jewish Affairs*, 52(2), Winter 1997.
4 SA Friends of Beth Hatefutsoth Country Communities Research Project, Johannesburg, 1992- . The research has identified 324 such country communities in South Africa. Figures as at April 2002.
5 Shain, Prof. Milton, in an interview 29.3.1990.
6 Uys, 'Die Jode van Namakwaland'.
7 This spread of occupations conforms to the recent findings of Gwynne Schrire in her article 'Mostly Smouse? – South African Jews and Their Occupations a Century Ago', *Jewish Affairs*, Pesach 2000.
8 Interview with Colla Swart, a native Namaqualander, n.d.

2 A Timeless landscape

1 Steenkamp, Willem, *Land of the Thirst King*, Cape Town, 1975, p.23.
2 Reid, Prof. Dave, Department of Geological Sciences, University of Cape Town, in an interview with Adrienne Folb, 31 July 1996.
3 Term used by Simon van der Stel in his diary to describe the Copper Mountain where he discovered copper in 1685. The site of his excavations has been preserved as a national monument today and is near the present day Carolusberg copper mine.
4 *Simon van der Stel's Journal of his Expedition to Namaqualand 1685-1686*, edited by G Waterhouse, Dublin, 1932 referring to Olaf Berg's expedition.
5 Ibid.
6 Steenkamp, *Land of the Thirst King*, p.40.
7 *Simon van der Stel's Journal*, pp. 128 & 129.
8 Gordon, Robert Jacob, *Cape Travels*, 1777 to 1786, vol. 2, edited by Peter E Raper and Maurice Boucher, Johannesburg, 1988.
9 Ibid. 'Gordon named the Gariep the 'Orange' after William V and the ruling house of the United Netherlands, the House of Orange', p.126.
10 It is believed they have a common origin. Van Aswegen, H J, *History of South Africa to 1854*, Pretoria, 1990.
11 Tucker, A W, 'Richtersveld – the land and its people', public lecture delivered at Johannesurg 31 March 1913.
12 The Orange River is considered a 'frontier zone'. *Einiqualand – Studies of the Orange River Frontier*, edited by Andrew B Smith, Cape Town, 1995.
13 Elphick, Richard, *Khoikhoi and the founding of White South Africa*, Johannesburg, 1985, p.10-22.
14 van Aswegen, *History of South Africa*, p. 24.
15 Penn, Nigel, 'Namaqualand and the northwestern Cape frontier zone c. 1650-1800', talk given to UCT Summer School in course 'Namaqualand: the neglected land', January 1991.
16 The Church followed the free burghers as they spread out into the interior but the Namaqualand church was only established much later, in 1850. Refer *NG Kerk 350*, ed George Hofmeyer, Lux Verbi.BM, 2002.
17 Penn, 'Namaqualand & the northwestern Cape'; *see also* Gordon, for painting of Ellenboogfontein in Little Namaqualand, p.255.
18 Steenkamp, *Land of the Thirst King*, p. 115.
19 Note that the Dutch Reformed Church missionaries only came later, the first missionary being appointed in 1860. *Die Gemeente Namakwaland* by Dr T N Hanekom, 1950 pp 82 & 144.
20 Emil Boonzaaier has offered another motive for such invitations. He suggests, that, rather than spiritual leadership for Coloured communities, 'the establishment of the mission stations provided the basters and the Khoikhoi with an effective safeguard against the encroaching Boers.' Boonzaaier, E A, 'Social Differentiation in the Richtersveld a Namaqualand Rural Area', (M A Social Anthropology thesis, University of Cape Town, 1980), p.77.
21 The mission stations at Komaggas and Steinkopf were recognised by the Colonial Government in 1843 and the other mission stations shortly after 1847 when the territory from the Buffels River to the Orange River was annexed and became Crown land. Tickets of Occupation recognised the indigenous population's right to use the land although they were denied mineral rights. By 1874 Komaggas, Leliefontein and Steinkopf had been granted Tickets of Occupation.
22 Dunne, Janeen, 'Towards A Regional Development Strategy For Namaqualand', Saldru Working Paper no. 75, Cape Town, 1988.
23 Field cornetcy – a designated area under the jurisdiction of the field cornet who maintained law and order in the Cape Government. In 1850 the Field Cornetcy of Namaqualand fell under the Division of Clanwilliam.
24 Copy of Option, Jowell collection.
25 Prior to the discovery at Springbokfontein, Thomas Fanin, on behalf of the S A Mining Company, had attempted to mine copper in the Richtersveld, but labour and transport proved too problematic. Smalberger, John M, *A History of Copper Mining in Namaqualand*, Cape Town, 1975, p. 28.
26 Wyley, Andrew, *Cape of Good Hope Report upon the Mineral and Geological Structure of South Namaqualand and the Adjoining Mineral Districts*, Cape Town,1857, Appendix, pp. 35-55.
27 Cape Almanac, 1856.
28 The first meeting of the newly constituted Namaqualand Divisional Council was held on 19 February 1861.

3 The first entrepreneur

1 Abrahams, Israel, *The Birth of a Community*, Cape Town, 1955.
2 Herrman, Louis, *The Jews in South Africa*, London, 1930.
3 Neethling, J H, 'Wheat Varieties in South Africa. Their history and development until 1912', Union of SA, Dept of Agriculture, 1932, Science Bulletin no.108, Stellenbosch, Scientific Bulletin, Series no. 13.
4 Thomson, George, *Travels and Adventure in Southern Africa*, edited by Vernon S Forbes, Cape Town, 1967.
5 Cape of Good Hope, *Report from the Select Committee appointed to report upon the Construction of Railways in the Colony*, 14 September 1854, p.4 .
6 C O 4071, Ref. 6, 19 September 1853.
7 E A Judge Papers, BC 500, Manuscripts and Archives Dept., UCT Libraries.
8 Saron, Gustav & Hotz, Louis, *The Jews in South Africa*, Cape Town, 1955, p.11.
9 Aaron de Pass Journal. Rebecca Walker Collection, Northamptonshire, England. The Journal consists primarily of a chronicle of events in his life.

4 Sugar, Soap and Velskoene

1 Joseph Sherman in *From a Land Far Off: South African Yiddish stories in English translation*, Cape Town, 1987, p.5 writes: 'The common roots of both Afrikaans and Yiddish gave each language a familiar ring to the speakers of the other, and each found it easy to acquire.'

2 Romm, Ittamar Chaim 'What Is a Smous', *SA Jewish Times*, Rosh Hashanah, September 1985.
3 Uys, 'Die Jode van Namakwaland'.
4 Ibid.
5 'the one flourishing business'.
6 *Die Gemeente Namakwaland, 'n Eeufees-Gedenkboek 1850-1950*, edited Dr T N Hanekom, 1950 referring to ds. W J Conradie's observations in Ondervindingen van een jonge Predikant in Namakwaland, p. 94 Translation: 'Pray for us and we will look after you'.
7 Inquest Report, Springbokfontein, 16.11.1898 on death of Abraham Jowell, trader. 1/SBK 3/1/2 Inquests Jan. 1897-Dec. 1900.
8 Smalberger, *A History of Copper Mining*, pp. 94-95.
9 The land of kaross or skinwearer.
10 Backhouse, James. *A Narrative of a Visit to the Mauritius and South Africa*, Hamilton, 1844, p.581.
11 Cape of Good Hope Blue Book, 1904.
12 Steenkamp, Ds L M, 'Samevattende Geskiedenis van Garies', opgestel ten tyde van die Van Riebeeck-feesviering en oorhandig aan die Poskoets te Garies op Maandag, 17 Maart 1952.
13 'far-flung community', *Die Gemeente Namakwaland*, p. 83.
14 Steenkamp, 'Samevattende Geskiedenis'.
15 Ibid., 'water from the roof'.
16 Ibid.
17 Uys, 'Die Jode van Namakwaland'.
18 Ibid.
19 Horwitz, Ralph, 'The Crumbling of Apartheid: the triumph of Capitalism', unpublished manuscript, 1993.

5 Commandeered into War

1 Nasson, Bill, *The South African War 1899-1902*, London, 1999, p.xi.
2 Burke, Peter, *The Siege of O'okiep*, Bloemfontein, 1995, p.7.
3 Saks, David Y, articles in *Jewish Affairs* Summer 1996 and Spring 1997.
4 Saks, David Y, 'Jews on Commando' *Jewish Affairs*, Spring 1999.
5 Boer War Memorial, 1897, 1898, 1899, 1/SBK/5/3/4 Ref. 556.
6 Ibid.
7 Burke, *The Siege of O'okiep*, p.14.
8 Ibid., p.55.
9 CO 8561 Ref. 22, 19.1.1903.
10 Burke, *The Siege of O'okiep.*
11 Reitz, Deneys, *Commando, a Boer Journal of the Boer War*, London, 1929, p.278.
12 Cape Archives, 1/SPK 4/9/7 772.660/02, dated 19.05.1902.
13 Nasson, Bill, *Abraham Esau's War: a black South African War in the Cape*, 1991, p.108.
14 Register of Prospectors, 1892, 1/ SBK 8/1/1.
15 Licensing Court Papers January 1905, 1/SBK 8/1/2, review of applications for retail wine and spirit licenses from Garies Hotel and Mr Burke of Garies; Joseph Schur of Bowesdorp; Bennett and Webster of O'okiep; John Louis de Oliviera of Springbokfontein and in 1907 renewal of license of A J Loynes of Springbokfontein.

6 Shopkeepers and Hoteliers

1 Meyer, G, *Uit die Verre Noordwester*, Cape Town, 1960.
2 *SA Jewish Chronicle*, 30.10.1908, p.239.
3 Interview with Esther Caplan, wife of Victor, 21.8. 1991.
4 1918 total population figures not available. Figures for white population were 6 327. There are no official census figures for the year 1911. Cape of Good Hope Census Report, 1904; UG 19/20, 1918 Census Namaqualand.
5 They would have sowed but not harvested.
6 Leveson, Marcia, 'Jewish Hoteliers of the SA Country Communities' – talk given to SA Friends of Beth Hatefutsoth public evenings, Cape Town, March 1990.
7 Licensing Court Papers: Applications for retail wine and spirit licenses. 1/SBK 8/1/2.
8 Birkby, Carel, *Thirstland Treks*, London, 1936, p. 91.
9 Lidded trunk-like rectangular boxes with side handles used for transporting merchandise.
10 Schapera, Abe. 'Golden Days in Namaqualand', unpub., Cape Town, 1969.

7 Life in the Bundu

1 Interview with Sidney Windisch, October 1986.
2 Talk given by Marian van Niekerk, wife of the district surgeon, Dr Izak van Niekerk, to a group of women in Nababeep, the 'NamaMamas' circa 1950s, on life in Namaqualand in the first two decades of the twentieth century.
3 Leveson, Dr Marcia, 'Jewish Hoteliers of the Country', talk given to SA Friends of Beth Hatefutsoth, Cape Town, 22.5.2000.
4 Birkby, *Thirstland Treks*, p.92.
5 Raphael Schapera interview, 27 September 1993.
6 Interview Dan Rabie, who lived in Namaqualand from 1910 – 1921. Kaplan Oral History Project, Manuscripts & Archives Dept., UCT Libraries, BC 949.
7 Rabinowitz, Isobel, 'King Solomon of the Richtersveld', unpublished manuscript, n.d.
8 Kaplan Oral history Project, BC 949.
9 In a Jewish traditional home, the kitchen is cleaned and crockery, cutlery and utensils cleaned or changed for the Festival of Passover.
10 Abe Schapera lived in Bowesdorp and Springbok between 1921 and 1934.

8 Milestones and dust storms

1 *An Illustrated History of South Africa*, edited by Trewhella Cameron, Johannesburg, 1986, pp 231-238.
2 Springbok Brochure, 1952, p.20, Piet van Heerde collection, Cape Archives.
3 Piet van Heerde has listed the years of severe droughts: 1895, 1896, 1907, 1919 (and later in 1924, 1927 and 1933).
4 Marais, Jan, resident geologist of the O'okiep Copper Company, 'Namaqualand – where it all began 300 years ago' – extract from manuscript, SA Mining, Coal, Gold and Base Minerals, October 1985.
5 Property of Mrs Douglas Cornell, daughter-in-law of Fred Cornell. First verse of poem.
6 Official census figures. At that stage the electoral boundaries of Namaqualand still included the Vanrhynsdorp area.
7 *The South African Jewish Chronicle*, 30/10/1908, p.239.
8 *The Standard Jewish Encyclopedia*, ed. Cecil Roth, London, 1966.
9 Shimoni, Gideon, *Jews and Zionism: The South African Experience 1910-1967*, Cape Town, 1980.
10 Lilian Dubb in a letter to Larna Bronstein, the librarian of the SA Friends of Beth Hatefutsoth, 20 June 1996.
11 Ds Willem Petrus Steenkamp became spiritual head of the diocese of Namaqualand in 1919 and motivated for the building of the central church in Springbok. He left Namaqualand in 1923 and, with his son, studied medicine in Europe. In 1929, now as Dr Steenkamp, he was elected Member of Parliament for Namaqualand. (*Die Gemeente Namakwaland*, pp 111-118).
12 *Die Gemeente Namakwaland*, p. 86.
13 Gordon, Tilly, Unpublished Memoirs, Jowell private collection.
14 Schapera, 'Golden Days in Namaqualand'.
15 Kotze, P W, *Sosiologiese Studie van 'n Geisoleerde Gemeenskap*, Kaapstad, 1943, p. 217.
16 Schapera, 'Golden Days in Namaqualand'.
17 Recently published by Jopie Kotze of the Springbok Lodge, Springbok (Jopie Kotze is a third generation Namaqualander and very interested in the early history of the village, particularly the Jewish community). Schapera, A, *Golden Days in Namaqualand*, Springbok, 2001.
18 strange horse.
19 Schapera, 'Golden Days in Namaqualand'.
20 Kotze, *Sosiologiese Studie*, p. 217.
21 Population Census Ref 02-02-01, 1904-1960.
22 3/SBK vol. 1. Springbok Village Management Board, Minutes, Nov. 1922- Sept. 1929 .

9 The Lure of Diamonds

1 Rabinowitz, 'King Solomon of the Richtersveld'.
2 Ibid.
3 Ibid.
4 Diamonds had been discovered in the vicinity of Luderitzbucht in 1908, after which Dr Merensky pointed to possibilities in the area south of Luderitzbucht to the Orange River. Using camels, geologists George Klinghardt and Ernest Reuning carried out prospecting work on the northern bank of the Orange River but failed to find any diamonds there at that time.
5 Carstens, Jack, *A Fortune Through My Fingers*, Cape Town, 1962, p.47.
6 Green, Lawrence G, *On Wings of Fire*, Cape Town, 1982.
7 Carstens, *A Fortune Through My Fingers*, p. 58.
8 Reuning, E 'The Discovery of Namaqualand Diamonds', *Mining and Industrial Magazine of Southern Africa*, 12 December 1928.
9 Rudd, B J and Watson V U T, *History of Namaqualand Diamond Discoveries*, Johannesburg, 1956.
10 Lehman Olga, *Look Beyond the Wind: The Life of Dr Hans Merensky*, Cape Town, 1955.
11 Carstens, *A Fortune Through My Fingers*, p.135.
12 Lehman, *Look Beyond the Wind.*
13 Rabinowitz, 'King Solomon of the Richtersveld'.
14 Aschman, George, 'A Jewish Prospector', *Hasholom Rosh Hashonah Annual*, September 1933, p. 39.
15 got nothing.
16 Carstens, *A Fortune Through My Fingers*, p.135.
17 Erasmus, B P J, *On Route in South Africa*, Johannesburg, 1995.

10 Lots to celebrate

1 'Motoring as Namaqualand's Newest Industry,' *The Cape Argus*, November 19, 1929.
2 The District record book, Magistrates office, Springbok, 5 April 1989 shows 8 018 whites, 15 139 Coloureds and 194 blacks in Namaqualand in 1931.
3 Schapera, Abe, 'Judaism in Namaqualand', unpublished manuscript, 'At a conservative estimate I venture to assess that during the vintage years of Jewry in Namaqualand (1920-1930) there must have been a total of not less than 200 Jews'.
4 1926 Census, UG 37-29.
5 Norwich, R, 'Synagogues on the Witwatersrand and Pretoria before 1932: their origin, form and function', (M.Arch. thesis, University of the Witwatersrand, 1988).
6 Namaqualand Hebrew Congregation Minute Book 1929-1972, Manuscripts and Archives Dept., UCT Libraries
7 Ibid.
8 Namaqualand Hebrew Congregation Minute Book, AGM 25 November 1934.
9 'tickets for our church'.
10 'We will buy a ticket, but not to dance, to enjoy the delicious food'.
11 Women's Agricultural Association.

11 Darker Times

1 Uys, 'Die Jode van Namakwaland', 'a few shillings for church money'.
2 Ibid., 'a packet of sweets as a gift'.
3 Ibid., 'a very good person'.
4 Ibid., 'He extended credit to them during difficult times and did more than his share for the poor and needy in his part of the world.'
5 Interview with Dave Teperson, Israel, 1986.
6 Schapera, 'Golden Days in Namaqualand'.
7 'In no other district was the relationship between the Jewish community and the Christian as good as in these parts.'
8 Hanekom, *Die Gemeente Namakwaland*, p. 183.
9 'Now why don't we build a little lorry?'
10 'but Alice is a girl's name'.
11 'smacked'.
12 'in this classroom it is pronounced "kway" '.
13 James Roux Papers . Jowell Private Collection. Translation 'totally destructive drought'.
14 van der Merwe, Dr PJ, *Pioniers van die Dorsland*, Cape Town, 1949 pp. 93 & 94.
15 O'Meara, Dan, *Volkskapitalisme – Class, Capital and Ideology in the Development of Afrikaner Nasionalism*, 1934-1948, Johannesburg, 1986, p. 16.
16 Shain, Milton, *The Roots of Anti-Semitism in South Africa*, Johannesburg, 1994, p. 115.
17 Ibid., p. 129.
18 Ibid., p. 137-41.
19 Ibid., p. 143.
20 SA Friends of Beth Hatefutsoth, Country Communities Research Project, 2000.
21 Ibid.
22 church organs.
23 Dwolatsky, Jack, Country Organiser for the SA Jewish Board of Deputies, February 1940.
24 SA Friends of Beth Hatefutsoth, Country Communities Research Project, 2000.

12 Life at the Coast

1 Lees, Robin, *Fishing for Fortunes: the Story of the Fishing Industry in Southern Africa, and the Men who Made it*, Cape Town, 1969.
2 Ibid.
3 Green, *On Wings of Fire*, p.57.

13 Declining Years

1 Uys, 'Die Jode van Namakwaland'.
2 Ibid.
3 *Copper-Nama News*, 6(11), July 1970.
4 'true Afrikaners'.
5 literally means 'to health', used as a toast but in this instance, means a drink at the hotel after synagogue services on Friday nights.
6 Duchinsky, Rabbi E J, *Report on Country Communities*, Johannesburg, 1964.
7 SA Mining, Coal, Gold and Base Minerals, October 1985, extract from a manuscript compiled by Jan Marais, resident geologist of the O'okiep Copper Company, on the discovery and development of minerals in Namaqualand, 1985.
8 Kotze, G, Interview, Springbok, 1991.
9 *SA Jewish Times*, 16 August 1963, p. 6.

Medical research takes them back ▶

Isobel Edelstein (*née* Sovinsky), as a social worker, was part of the medical team from Groote Schuur Hospital, Cape Town, that conducted a genealogical study in Namaqualand in the 1960s into a rare disease, lipoid proteinosis. Here she is shown enlisting the ubiquitous donkey to help pull their car out of the sand near Steinkopf.

ACKNOWLEDGEMENTS

This book has been ten years in the making. It emanated from a family history and the story burst at the seams until we gave it its rightful place as a fully-fledged social history, capturing the spirit of the lives and times of some of Namaqualand's remarkable inhabitants. Through each of those ten years we have encountered many people whose involvement ultimately enriched this project. Without them, we could never have traipsed this dusty path. While we will endeavour to mention each of them by name, there are some to whom we wish to extend a special thanks for their ongoing and unwavering support:

To the person who turned multiple scraps of paper into categorised order – Pam Kolbe, patient and tenacious librarian. She has assisted us for over ten years, often travelling out of her way to work with us. After so much time together, and being neither Namaqualander nor Jewish, we imagine that she is now part both!
To Arlene Fanaroff, dedicated researcher who was always prepared to run with wild ideas and find ways to implement them.
To Charles Maggs, our talented young book designer who brought a fresh air of creativity to a very old subject!
To Pieter and Pam Struik, our publishers and a most outstanding team who are always keen supporters of our projects. Pieter's professionalism, vision and direction kept us focussed and striving for excellence.
To Leonie Twentyman Jones, our extremely able editor who has a long-standing connection with our projects and is always a pleasure to work with.
To Marian Robertson, social history researcher with a wealth of knowledge into which we were privileged to tap.
To Jopie Kotze, an old friend whose personality colours these pages as a Namaqualand resident and local history enthusiast.
To Ruth Rosen, the best of friends who was even willing to conduct research in London on our behalf.
And to Joanne Jowell, published author, editor and great supporter of this project.

We would also like to express our sincerest thanks and gratitude to the following:

Roger Bell, photographer; Veronica Belling, Jewish Studies Library, UCT Libraries; Paula Berman, editing; Kathy Brookes, MuseumAfrika; Harry Bouwers, Namaqualand today; Cape Archives; Mrs Douglas Cornell, poem; Christo De Wit, Namaqualand today; Sally Frankental, guidance; Irene Friedland, research; Lesley Hart and staff, Manuscripts and Archives, UCT Libraries; Ralph Horwitz, economic theory; Junaid Jacobs, Diatype setting; Maggi Joseph, Namaqualand research; Neil Jowell, original journals; Gerry Levin, geologist; Kowie Lombard, Springbok agricultural history; Jackie Loos, research; Jan Marais, geology material; Marshay McKay, computer expertise; Dr Duncan Miller, archaeological metallurgist; Norman Morrison, great help in every direction; Frankie Myers, Namaqualand material; National Library of South Africa, Cape Town branch; Steve Phelps, loan of diamond material; Milly Pimstone, read-through; Dr David L Reid, Namaqualand geology; Dr Graham Ross, sharing his Namaqualand research and photographs; James and Esther Roux, Namaqualand farming history; SA Friends of Beth Hatefutsoth Country Communities Research Project; Colla Swart, Kamieskroon; Milton Shain, UCT Kaplan Centre for Jewish Studies, guidance; Phillida Brooke Simons; Springbok Municipality; Rey van Rensburg, Namaqualand today; Glen von Zeil; Phoebe Walker, UK, material on De Pass family; Rebecca Walker, UK, De Pass history; Marcelle Weiner, Brenthurst Press, historical material; Betty Wright, wonderful Namaqualand material.

A special thanks to Jeanette Marcus for her loving support throughout this project and to Lilian Matthews who kept us going with lots of good food.

GLOSSARY

Aanneming (Afrikaans) confirmation
Atjar (Persian origin) a hot pickle or relish of fruit or vegetables
Baleboste (Yiddish) capable woman
Barmitzvah (Hebrew) ceremony when a boy reaches his thirteenth birthday
Baroof (Yiddish) occupation or career
Beth Din (Hebrew) Jewish ecclesiastical court
Boerbrood (Afrikaans) home-made brown bread
Boere Jode (Afrikaans) literally 'Jewish farmers' – Jews who were considered 'real Afrikaners'
Bokmis (Afrikaans) goat dung
Bris or brith milah (Hebrew) circumcision
Bundu (Shona) wild open country, remote from civilization
Burger (Afrikaans) citizen. Free burgers were European employees of the Dutch East India Company whose contracts with the Company had been terminated to allow them to operate as farmers
Bywoner (Afrikaans) share-cropper working part of another person's land
Challah (Hebrew) plaited bread baked for the Sabbath
Chazzan (Hebrew) cantor
Cheder (Hebrew) elementary Hebrew school originating in Eastern Europe
CID (English abbreviation) Criminal Investigation Department
Dassie (Afrikaans) rock rabbit
Dominee (Afrikaans) minister
Dorp (Afrikaans) village
Eeufees (Afrikaans) centenary celebrations
Geselskap (Afrikaans) conversation
Haggadah (Hebrew) Book of the Story of Exodus
Handlen (Yiddish) compare 'handel' (Afrikaans) commerce, trade, business
Homentashen (Yiddish) cakes specially baked for the festival of Purim
IDB (English abbreviation) Illicit Diamond Buying
Kaross (Khoi) a blanket or clothing made of skins from animals such as sheep, goats, jackal, lynx, wild cat and dassie
Kashrut (Hebrew) religious requirements, particularly pertaining to dietary laws and food preparation
Kerkie (Afrikaans) little church
Kerkorrels (Afrikaans) church organs
Kiddush wine (Hebrew) ceremonial wine
Klapped (Afrikaans) slapped
Klip-doktor (Afrikaans) stone doctor
Klipkerk (Afrikaans) stone church
Kloof (Afrikaans) ravine
Koppie (Afrikaans) hillock
Kosher (Hebrew) complying with Jewish Religious Laws, especially the Dietary laws
Kraalbos (Afrikaans) indigenous bush
Lapgat (Afrikaans) patched
Matjieshuis (Afrikaans) hut made of reeds
Matzoth (Hebrew) 'unleavened bread' eaten during Passover
Mekler (Yiddish) agent or salesman
Middelmannetjie (Afrikaans) a continuous hump between the wheel ruts in an untarred road or track
Minyan (Hebrew) ten men needed for a synagogue service
Mohel (Hebrew) person who performs the circumcision
Mon (Yiddish) poppy seed
Nagmaal (Afrikaans) the sacrament of Holy Communion celebrated quarterly in the Dutch Reformed Church; an occasion when large numbers of country people visited the towns.
Oude kerkie (Afrikaans) the old little church
Pakke (Afrikaans) suits
Parnas (Hebrew) synagogue dignitary
Parsha (Hebrew) portion of the law
Pesach/Passover (Hebrew) Jewish Festival commemorating the Exodus from Egypt
Platteland (Afrikaans) country or rural regions
Pogroms (Russian) persecutions
Poor white (English) someone who has become dependent to such an extent, that he is unfit, without help from others, to find a proper means of livelihood
Purim (Hebrew) Jewish Festival commemorating the rescue of Persian Jewry
Rokke (Afrikaans) dresses
Rosh Hashanah (Hebrew) Jewish New Year
Rummy (English) card game
SACS (English abbreviation) South African College School
SANTA (English abbreviation) South African National Tuberculosis Association
SAWAS (English abbreviation) South African Women's Auxiliary Service
Schenodering book (Yiddish) donations book
Schmoozing (Yiddish) a friendly, gossipy conversation
Schochet (Hebrew) ritual slaughterer
Seder (Hebrew) home ceremony Passover festival
Sefer Torah (Hebrew) Scroll of Law
Shammash (Hebrew) beadle
Shtetlekh (Yiddish) villages
Shul (Yiddish) synagogue
Sink (Afrikaans) corrugated iron
Smous (Afrikaans) hawker or itinerant pedlar
Stoep (Afrikaans) a raised platform or verandah in front of or all round a house
Succoth (Hebrew) temporary dwelling with a roof of branches, partially open to the sky, used for meals during the festival of Sukkot (Tabernacles)
Tannie-doktor (Afrikaans) woman with experience of home remedies
Togger(s) (Afrikaans) itinerant pedlar(s)
Trekboere (Afrikaans) nomadic stock farmers, who grazed their stock further and further inland
Trekbokken (Afrikaans) springbok migrations
Veld (Afrikaans) countryside, landscape
Velskoene (Afrikaans) home-made shoes
VLV (Afrikaans) Vroue Landbou Vereniging / Women's Agricultural Association
Voortrekker (Dutch) Afrikaner frontier farmers who left the Cape Colony between 1834 and 1840 in an organized migration (Great Trek) to establish new states in the interior where they would be free of British rule.
Wagters (Yiddish) men who stay with the deceased's body until the burial
WIZO (English abbreviation) Women's International Zionist Organization
Yiddishe Nagmaal (Afrikaans) Jewish version of Holy Communion
Yom Ha'atzmaut (Hebrew) anniversary of the establishment of the State of Israel
Yom Kippur (Hebrew) Day of Atonement
Yomtov (Hebrew) religious festival
Zionist (English) movement to secure the Jewish return to the land of Israel

BIBLIOGRAPHY

Manuscript Sources

Aaron de Pass Journal, Rebecca Walker Collection, Northamptonshire, England

Cornelissen, Alwyn, Namaqualand Copper History, unpublished papers, 1965

Gordon, Julius, 'Springbok, Namaqualand', unpublished, Springbok, 1924

Gordon, Tilly, 'Memoirs', unpublished, n.d.

Horwitz, Ralph, 'The Crumbling of Apartheid: the Triumph of Capitalism', unpublished manuscript, 1993

Horwitz, Ralph, 'Smous and Darwin', unpublished manuscript, n.d.

Rabinowitz, Isabel, 'King Solomon of the Richtersveld' unpublished manuscript, n.d.

Schapera, Abe, 'Golden Days in Namaqualand', unpublished manuscript, 1969

Schapera, Abe, 'Judaism in Namaqualand', unpublished manuscript, n.d.

Sketchbook of visit to Kings Mine c 1852, Mendelssohn Collection, Library of Parliament, Cape Town

Steenkamp, Ds. L. M., 'Samevattende Geskiedenis van Garies', unpublished, 1952

Uys, Theunis, 'Die Jodemense van Namakwaland: Hulle Invloed op Kulturele, Maatskaplike en Ekonomiese Gebied', unpublished manuscript, 2003

Springbok

District Record Book, Springbok, Magistrate's Office, 5 April 1929

Cape Archives

Springbok, Namaqualand Magistracy

1/SBK 3/1/2 Inquests January 1897-December 1900

1/SBK 5/3/4, 1897-1899 Boer War memorial no. 556

1/SBK 8/1/2 Licensing Court Papers. Applications for retail wine and spirit licences, January 1905

3/SBK vol.1 Springbok Village Management Board. Minutes November 1922-September 1929

Colonial Office

CO 8561, Ref. 22, 19.01.1903, Office of the Civil Commissioner & Resident Magistrate of Namaqualand. Correspondence

Accession

Piet van Heerde Collection

National Library of South Africa, Cape Town branch

Moffatt, H.R., Collection

University of Cape Town Libraries

Judge, E.A. Family Papers. Manuscripts and Archives BC 500

Namaqualand Hebrew Congregation Minute Book 1929-1972

Rabie, Dan, Interview. Kaplan Oral History Project BC 949

Books, pamphlets, articles and theses

Abrahams, Professor Rabbi Israel, *The Birth of a Community*, Cape Town, 1955

Alexander, James Edward, *An Expedition of Discovery into the Interior of Africa in two volumes*, Facsimile reprint, Cape Town, 1967

Aschman, George, 'A Jewish Prospector' *Hasholom Rosh Hashonah Annual*, September 1933

Backhouse, James, *A Narrative of a Visit to the Mauritius and South Africa*, Hamilton, 1844

Birkby, Carel, *Thirstland Treks*, London, 1936

Boonzaaier, E.A., 'Social Differentiation in the Richtersveld, a Namaqualand Rural Area', MA thesis (Social Anthropology), University of Cape Town, 1980

Burke, Peter, *The Siege of O'Okiep*, Bloemfontein, 1995

Cameron, Trewhella, ed., *An Illustrated History of South Africa*, Johannesburg, 1986

Carstens, Jack, *A Fortune Through My Fingers*, Cape Town, 1962

Christen, Leunende, *Waar die Kokerboom Luister: 'n Lewenskets van Dr. Izak van Niekerk van Namakwaland*, Stellenbosch, 1948

Conradie, W.J., *Ondervinden van Een Jonge Predikant in Namakwaland*, London, 1909

Cornell, Fred C., *The Glamour of Prospecting*, London, 1920

Consolidated Diamond Mines, 'Diamonds from the Desert', Brochure, 1956

Cullinan, Patrick, *Robert Jacob Gordon 1743-1795. The Man and his Travels at the Cape*, Cape Town, 1992

'The Dembitzer Story', *The Copper Chronicle*, Nababeep, December 1972, 2 (4)

Dickason, Graham B., *Cornish Immigrants to South Africa*, Cape Town, 1978

Duchinsky, Rabbi E.J., *Survey and Report on Country Communities*, Johannesburg, 1964

Dunne, Janeen, 'Towards Regional Strategy for Namaqualand', South African Labour and Development Research Unit, Working Paper no. 75, Cape Town, 1988

Eliavson, Sima, *Namaqualand in Flower*, Johannesburg, 1972

Elphick, Richard, *Khoikhoi and the Founding of White South Africa*, Johannesburg, 1985

Erasmus, B. P. J., *On Route in South Africa*, Johannesburg, 1995

Forbes, Vernon S., *Pioneer Travellers in South Africa*, Cape Town, 1965

Forbes, Vernon S. and Rourke, John, *Paterson's Cape Travels 1777-1779*, Johannesburg, 1980

Forsyth, Don K., 'Medal for the Defence of O'okiep 4 April – 4 May 1902', The Cape Copper Co., n.d.

Fraser, Gill, 'Ovenstones, a Story of the Sea', Cape Town, 1958

Giliomee, Hermann, *The Afrikaners, biography of a people*, Cape Town, 2003

Green, Lawrence G., *On Wings of Fire*, Cape Town, 1982

Green, Lawrence G., *So Few are Free*, Cape Town, 1983

Green, Lawrence G., *To the Rivers End*, Cape Town, 1981

Hanekom, Dr. T.N., *Die Gemeente Namakwaland. 'n Eeufees-Gedenkboek (1850-1950)*, Cape Town, 1950

Herrman, Louis, *The Jews in South Africa*, London, 1930

Jowell, Phyllis, *Joe Jowell of Namaqualand*, Cape Town, 1994

Kaplan, Mendel, *From Shtetl to Steelmaking*, Cape Town, 1979

Kaplan, Mendel, *Jewish Roots in the South African Economy*, Cape Town, 1986

Kaplan, Mendel and Robertson, Marian eds., *Founders and Followers*, Cape Town, 1991

Kotze, P.W., *Sosiologiese Studie van 'n Geisoleerde Gemeenskap*, Cape Town, 1943

L'Ange, Gerald, *Urgent Imperial Service. South African Forces in German South West Africa 1914-15*, Rivonia, 1991

Le Vaillant, Francois, *Travels in South Africa 1781-1784*, 2v, Cape Town, 1973

Lees, Robin, *Fishing for Fortunes. The Story of the Fishing Industry in Southern Africa – and the Men who Made It*, Cape Town, 1969

Lehman, Olga, *Look beyond the Wind: The Life of Dr Hans Merensky*, Cape Town, 1955

Letcher, Owen, 'Namaqualand. Cradle of Mineral Development in Southern Africa' Johannesburg, repr. from the *Mining and Industrial Magazine of Southern Africa*, 1932

Leveson, Marcia, 'Jewish Hoteliers of the South African Country Communities', Talk given to SA Friends of Beth Hatefutsoth, Cape Town, March 1990

Marais, Jan, *O'okiep Copper Company Ltd. 1937-1987*, Nababeep, 1987

Meyer, G., *Uit Die Verre Noordweste*, Cape Town, 1960

Miller, Dr Duncan, 'The Indigenous History of Non-Ferrous

Metal Production', Talk given to UCT Summer School at Iziko Museums, Cape Town, February 2002
Moffatt, Henry Robert, *Scenes and Services in South Africa: The Story of Robert Moffatt's Half-century of Missionary Labours*, London, 1876
'Motoring as Namaqualand's Newest Industry', Cape Town, *The Cape Argus*, 19 November, 1929
Municipality of Springbok, 'Springbok, Namaqualand Centenary Brochure', Cape Town, 1963
Murray, Marischal, *Ships and South Africa*, London, 1933
Nasson, W.R. *Abraham Esau's War: a black South African War in the Cape*, Cambridge, 1991
Nasson, W.R., *The South African War 1899-1902*, London, 1999
Neethling, Prof J. H., 'Wheat Varieties in South Africa. Their History and Development until 1912', Union of South Africa, Dept. of Agriculture. Government Printer 1932. Stellenbosch, Elsenberg College of Agriculture, Science Bulletin no.108 series13.
Nienaber, G.S. and Raper, P.E., *Toponymica Hottentotica*. Naamkundereeks No 7. Pretoria, 1977
Norwich, Oscar I. and Kolbe, Pam, *Maps of Africa*, Johannesburg, 1983
Norwich, Rose, 'Recording our Past', *Jewish Affairs*, 52(2), Winter 1997
Norwich, Rose, 'Synagogues on the Witwatersrand and Pretoria before 1932 – their origin, form and function', M.Arch thesis, University of the Witwatersrand, 1988
O'Meara, Dan, *Volkskapitalisme. Class, Capital and Ideology in the Development of Afrikaner Nationalism 1934-1948*, Johannesburg, 1983
Ogilvie, Ivan, 'Simon van der Stel and South Africa's First Copper Mine', *Optima*, September 1985
O'okiep Copper Mining Company Ltd., 'Namaqualand Copper 1852-1952', Brochure
Penn, Nigel, 'Namaqualand and the Northwestern Cape Frontier Zone', talk given to UCT Summer School, Cape Town, January 1991
Raper, Peter E. and Boucher, Maurice, eds., *Robert Jacob Gordon Cape Travels 1777-1786*, 2v. Johannesburg, 1988
Readers Digest Illustrated History of South Africa – the Real Story, Cape Town, 1988
Reitz, Denys, *Commando. A Boer Journal of the Boer War*, 2nd ed. London, 1983
Reuning, Dr. E., 'The Discovery of Namaqualand Diamonds', *Mining and Industrial Magazine of Southern Africa*, 12 December 1928
Romm, Ittamar Chaim, 'What is a Smous', *SA Jewish Times*, September 1985
Rudd, B.J. and Watson, V.U.T., *History of Namaqualand Diamond Discoveries*, Johannesburg, March 1956
Saks, David Y., 'Jews on Commando', *Jewish Affairs*, 54(3), Spring 1999
Saks, David Y., 'Three Boere-Jode on Commando', *Jewish Affairs*, 51(4), Summer 1996
Saron, Gustav and Hotz, Louis, *The Jews in South Africa*, Cape Town, 1955
Saunders, Christopher and Southey, Nicholas eds., *Historical Dictionary of South Africa*, 2nd ed., Metuchen, N.J., 2000
Schrire, Gwynne, 'Mostly Smouse – South African Jews and their Occupations a Century Ago', *Jewish Affairs*, 55(1), Pesach 2000
Scully, W.C., *Between Sun and Sand*, Cape Town, 1898
Scully, W.C., *The Wreck of the Grosvenor and other South African Poems*, Lovedale, 1886
Shain, Milton, *The Roots of Anti-Semitism in South Africa*, Johannesburg, 1994
Sherman, Joseph, ed., *From a Land Far Off: South African Yiddish stories in English translation*, Cape Town, 1987
Shimoni, G., *Jews and Zionism. The South African Experience 1910-1967*, Cape Town, 1980
Simon, Bishop M., *Bishop for the Hottentots: African Memoirs 1882-1909*, New York, 1959
Simons, Phillida Brooke, ed., *John Blades Currey. Fifty Years in the Cape Colony 1850-1900*, Johannesburg, 1986
Smalberger, John M., *A History of Copper Mining in Namaqualand 1846-1931*, Cape Town, 1975
Smith, Andrew B. ed., *Einiqualand – Studies of the Orange River Frontier*, Cape Town, 1995
Standard Encyclopaedia of South Africa, ed., by D.J. Potgieter and others, Goodwood, 1970-1976
Steenkamp, Willem, *Land of the Thirst King*, Cape Town, 1975
Thomson, George, *Travels and Adventure in Southern Africa*, ed. by Vernon Forbes, Cape Town, 1967
Tindall, Henry, *Two Lectures on Great Namaqualand and its Inhabitants*, Cape Town, 1856
Tucker, A. Winifred, *Richtersveld and its People*, Johannesburg, 1913
Van Aswegen, H.J., *History of South Africa to 1854*, Pretoria, 1990
Van der Merwe, P.J., *Pioniers van die Dorsland*, Cape Town, 1949
Van Heerde, Piet, and others, *Springbok Brochure 1952*, published for the van Riebeeck Festival celebrations, Springbok, 1952
Van Heerde, Louis, *Oom Piet van Heerde se Namakwalandse Fotoversameling, 1926-1979*, Springbok, 2001
Van Niekerk, Marian, 'Life in Namaqualand…', Talk given to the "NamaMamas" circa 1950's
Van Onselen, L.E., *Trekboer*, Cape Town, 1961
Waterhouse, Gilbert, ed., *Simon van der Stel's Journal of his Expedition to Namaqualand 1685-1686*, London, 1932
West, Martin, *Divided Community*, Cape Town, 1971

Newspapers and Periodicals

Cape Almanac
Cape Argus Nov 19 1929
Copper Chronicle 1972
Copper-Nama News July 1970
Die Suiderstem 12 May 1941
Elsenberg Agricultural College, Stellenbosch *Science Bulletin* no. 13
Jewish Affairs 1963, 1985, 1987, 1996, 1997, 1999, 2000
Optima September 1985
SA Jewish Chronicle 1908
SA Jewish Times 1963

Government Publications

Bell, Charles D., *Reports of the Surveyor-General on the Copper Fields of Little Namaqualand and of Commander M S Nolloth of HMS Frolic, on the Bays and Harbours of that Coast.* Cape Town, 1855, G.8-'55
Cape of Good Hope, *Report from the Select Committee appointed to report upon the Construction of Railways in this Colony*, 14 September, 1854, S.C.8-'54
Wyley, Andrew, *Report Upon the Mineral and Geological Structures of South Namaqualand and the Adjoining Mineral Districts*, Cape Town, 1857, G.36 –'57
Cape of Good Hope *Blue Book* 1904

INTERVIEWS AND PHOTOGRAPHS

We were able to develop this history because of the generosity shown by so many people who shared their memories and their family photographs with us.

Abramson, Dr Aubry
Berman, Harold
Bernstein, Sarah (Chloe) and Bernstein, Joyce
Block, Shirley
Boiskin, Morris
Boyd, Maxine
Caplan, Ellis
Caplan, Esther
Caplan, Florrie
Cohen, Marion
De Kock, Mary
Dembitzer, Max
Edelstein, Isobel
Faiman, Marion and Suttner, Hermione
Flax, Belle
Flax, Jeffrey and Barbara
Frank, Max
Galombik, Yvonne
Gelb, Beryl
Gelb, Raphael and Thelma
Gelb, Sue
Gomes, Mina and Kope, Freda
Gordon, Dr Hymie
Gordon, Selina
Gordon, Dr Walter
Grodd, Solly
Hardie, Lynette
Josman, Sonny and Pauline
Jowell, Bertha
Kluk, Solomon
Kotze, Gert
Levick, Riva and David
Levy, David
Lindenblutt, Doreen
Malherbe, Jacobus Petrus (Petrie)
Matheson, Cecily
Miller, Maureen
Nachman, Maureen
Neumann, Walter and Rosalyn
Pachter, Jack
Perel, Leona
Rabie, Dan
Rabie, Lulu and Merle
Rabie, Monty
Rabinowitz, Benjamin and Sylvia
Rabinowitz, Hyme
Rabinowitz, Joe
Rakoff, Cissie
Rakoff, Eugene
Rakoff, Prof Vivian
Rosenberg, Arthur, Valerie and Lynn
Rothschild, Pauline
Roux, James and Esther
Sacks, Marlene
Sadur, Doo
Sandler, Selina
Schapera, Dr Raphael
Schur, Clara
Sennett, Barbara
Sher, Monique and Yvette
Shulman, Reinet and Oscar
Silverman, Bella and Robert
Simanowitz, Dr Milton, UK
Simon, John
Slabbert, Brenda
Sovinsky, Sybil
Spector, Bernice
Teperson, Dave
Teperson, Monty
Udwin, Joyce
Uria, Marlin
Uys, Theunis and Hester
Van Heerde, Louis
Wilson, Kenneth
Windisch, Sidney
Witz, 'Stompie'

◀ Declining years

Approaching the Springbok Synagogue for the Mayoral Sunday Service, 1961.

A Namaqualander remembers

Sidney Windisch reminiscing with Adrienne Folb, 1991.
Folb collection

INDEX

Page numbers in italic refer to illustrations

Springbok in the 1920s
Painting by G W Pilkington

'Namaqualand on a hot day in a quiet town, the shade of the pepper tree and the still loneliness that pervades' (Hyme Rabinowitz) is an enduring memory.

FERNWOOD
PRESS

P O Box 15344, Vlaeberg 8018, South Africa
www.fernwoodpress.co.za

Registration no. 90/04463/07
First published 2004

Edited by Leonie Twentyman Jones
Designed by Charles Maggs and Stefanie Krieg-Elliott
Cartography by Red Roof Design
Dustjacket design by Willem Jordaan
Reproduction by Hirt & Carter, Cape Town
Printed and bound by Tien Wah Press (Pte) Ltd, Singapore

ISBN 1-874950-75-X